Mangiamo

MEDITERRANEAN
FAMILY RECIPES

Margie Raimondo

Copyright © 2022 Margie Raimondo

LIVING Water Books LLC
Christian Publishing House
640 Elsinger Blvd #1021
Conway, AR 72032
Livingwaterbooks.org

Print Book Edition 2022
Paperback - Hardcover - Digital
Library of congress cataloging in publication data available from the library of Congress.
ISBN 979-8-9868286-7-1

All rights reserved. In accordance with the U.S. Copyright Act of 1976, the scanning, uploading and electronic sharing of any part of the book without the author's permission constitute lawful piracy and theft and theft of the author's intellectual property. This book may not be copied or reprinted for commercial gain or profit. Any portion thereof may not be reproduced or used in any manner whatsoever without the express written permission of Margie Raimondo except for the use of brief quotations in a book review.

Ordering Information:
Quantity sales and special discounts are available on quantity purchases by corporations, associations, and others. For details, contact the author at the website below
www.urbanafarmstead.net

Printed in the United States of America
Living Water Books LLC Publishing
Cover Design
Editorial Director

Manufactured in The U.S

THE KITCHEN IS THE HEART OF THE HOME

"Cooking in our family is passed down from generation to generation. I hope Mangiamo brings the love and respect I have for our culture and cuisine to everyone's kitchen."

Chef Margie Raimondo

Many Italian recipes originate from a traditional culture of home cooking, using seasonal ingredients put together with minimal fuss. The daily ritual of visiting the market or picking from your garden for the freshest produce to cook; simply makes food an integral part of living. Growing up in an Italian household in an urban Southern Los Angeles neighborhood, my family converted the yard into a garden to grow our food. I grew up poor but never knew it because we always had fresh food on the table. The table is where we laughed, talked, and planned the next meal.

Over the years, I lived and traveled throughout several regions in Italy, where I learned to farm, harvest, and cook traditional Italian meals. Each experience taught me the important link between food and cultural heritage. Now, I never cook alone in my kitchen. I wrote this cookbook to share my love of family and food with you. All the recipes in *"Mangiamo"* celebrate fresh ingredients. I harness the flavors of global ingredients and infuse them with my Italian roots to create delicious meals that are always anchored in freshness, seasonality, and simplicity. Travel with me as we explore the world of food through recipes and stories. Experiment, be curious, be bold, and whatever you do, have fun!

MEDITERRANEAN FAMILY RECIPES

THE TABLE OF CONTENTS

THE KITCHEN IS THE HEART OF THE HOME	3
WHERE IT ALL BEGAN	6
ANTIPASTI E ZUPPA	7
PASTA E GNOCCHI	39
PANE E PIZZA	65
RICETTE DI FAMIGLIA SICILIANE	81
RICETTE DI FAMIGLIA NAPOLITANO	107
DOLCI	123
COOKING TECHNIQUES	
MEET THE CHEF	
SPECIAL THANKS	

WHERE IT ALL BEGAN

Family plays a central role in Italian traditions. The meals are relaxed affairs with several courses and may take hours. The goal is not just to eat -- it's time for the family members to converse and enjoy each other's company. Italy is historically divided into different regions, each with its own distinctive cuisine. Over time, influences such as spice traders from the Orient, the invading Greeks, and Saracens, as well as other countries' in close proximity to France, Spain, and Austria, have helped shape Italian home cooking into today's rich diversity.

The recipes are different depending on where you live. For example, pasta is pretty much all over but it is different everywhere. In the north, you have pasta alla Bolognese which is from Bologna or Carbonara, which is from Rome, or Pasta Alla Norma which is from Sicily. Mangiamo is a collection of recipes that reflects my father's Sicilian roots, my mother's Napolitano roots, and the peasant fare of my farm-stays in different regions of Italy. Each recipe is photographed with many useful hints on ingredients and techniques. Enjoy the step-by-step instructions and detailed methods I provide in creating these recipes within your home.

Antipasto is a traditional first course of an Italian meal. Literally, the word "antipasto" is derived from the Latin root "anti" meaning "before" and "pastus," which means "meal." Except for Sunday dinners and holidays, it is not an elaborate board of food like we imagine a charcuterie board. It is a plate with homemade sausage and cheese made by your family or a local farmer.

ANTIPASTI E ZUPPE

1

Campania, Italy

Sicily, Italy

MEAT ANTIPASTO

SERVES 6

Meat Antipasto called affettati misti (mixed cold cuts) in Italian, the platter should be made up of a good selection of meats that contrast in flavor and appearance. Cut the meat in different ways, for example sliced thin or cubed. Serve with fruit such as figs, olives and caperberries, or with slices of ripe melon or peaches.

INGREDIENTS

- 6 slices of lardo
- 6 slices salami
- 6 slices of coppa di parma
- 6 slices of bresaola
- 6 slices prosciutto
- 6 plain olive oil bruschetta (see page 23)
- 6 slices mortadella
- 6 chicken livers crostini (see page 18)
- Black olives, in brine and unpitted
- Cipollini (pickled baby onions)
- Caperberries
- Sun-dried tomatoes
- 3 figs
- 6 slices cantaloupe melon
- Country-style bread, such as ciabatta, to serve
- Extra virgin olive oil and lemon wedges.

INSTRUCTIONS

- Lay out the meat on a platter, folding some and rolling others. Arrange your accompaniments on the platter so your guests can help themselves.

- Always serve with plenty of bread, good extra virgin olive oil and lemon wedges.

Tip:
Always serve a meat antipasto platter at room temperature – meat taken straight from the refrigerator lacks flavor.

LEARNING
TECHNIQUE
Cuts

SHAVING

Some meats need to be shaved rather than sliced. Lardo is a piece of lard that has been salted, and sometimes flavored on the sides with herbs or spice. It should be shaved very finely with a cheese slicer, mandolin or potato peeler so it melts in the mouth, giving just a hint of flavor.

CUBING

Mortadella is my favorite. I like to cube Mortadella, a cooked sausage from Bologna. It is either very finely sliced and then rolled or folded or cut into cubes.

SLICING

Larger salami is best sliced on an electric slicer when you buy them. Smaller ones are okay to hand-slice.

Garnish and enjoy!

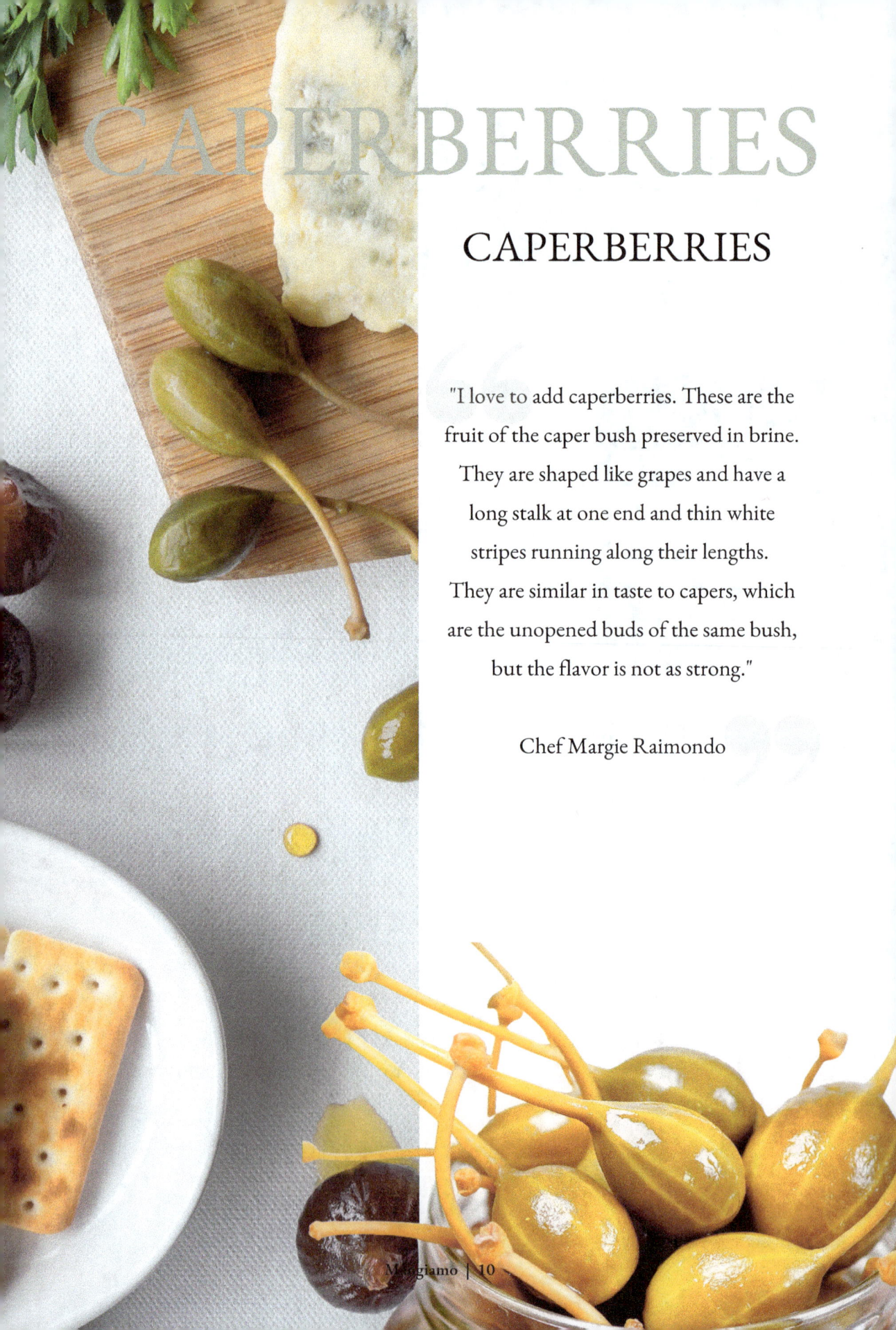

CAPERBERRIES

CAPERBERRIES

"I love to add caperberries. These are the fruit of the caper bush preserved in brine. They are shaped like grapes and have a long stalk at one end and thin white stripes running along their lengths. They are similar in taste to capers, which are the unopened buds of the same bush, but the flavor is not as strong."

Chef Margie Raimondo

SEAFOOD ANTIPASTO

Seafood Marinating Times

SERVES 4

I serve it during the holidays and for special Sunday meals. Even if you don't live on the coast, you can use a mix of local fish and store-bought fish and seafood. You can also buy marinated fish in jars or tins or from a local delicatessen.

Type	Marinating Time
Small-Medium Shrimp:	15 – 30 min
Large Shrimp:	30 – 45 min
Flaky Fish Filet:	30 min
Firm Fish Filet:	30 min – 1 hr
Firm Fish Steak:	1 – 2 hrs

Notes:

_____

_____

_____

_____

_____

COOKING INSTRUCTIONS

- Fresh broiled fish is one of the simplest and quickest antipasto to make at home. Heat the broiler and brush each fish with olive oil. Place a small slice of lemon in the cavity of the fish then broil the fish on both sides until cooked through.

Marinated with Olive Oil, Lemon, & Herbs

- Combine ½ cup olive oil, 2 tablespoons of fresh lemon juice (from 1 lemon), and fresh herbs (such as cilantro, basil, rosemary or thyme) removed from the stems and loosely chopped. Brush the marinade on the fish. Cover and chill for 10-25 minutes.

Marinated and Grilled

- When you prepare a seafood marinade, be sure to only use a small amount of an acidic ingredient with an oil based liquid. Don't leave the seafood in it for too long or the acid will start to cook the fish.

- Tip: It is difficult to brown seafood if the meat has too much water in it. Always pat fish filets and other seafood with paper towels before cooking to absorb any water on the skin. Excess water creates steam during cooking, preventing it from getting crisp, brown skin.

SHRIMP MARINATED
in Lime and Olive Oil

INGREDIENTS

- 1 pound of large shrimp
- 3 ½ teaspoons lime juice
- 2 tablespoons olive oil
- 1 tomato, seeded and cut into a ¼ inch dice
- ¼ teaspoon salt
- ⅛ teaspoon black pepper
- 2 tablespoons chopped parsley

INSTRUCTIONS

- Bring a pot of salted water to a boil. Add the shrimp, cover and bring back to a boil; partially cover for 1 to 2 minutes. Drain, let cool, and peel.

- In a large stainless steel bowl, combine the lime juice with oil, tomato, salt, pepper, and parsley.

- Add the shrimp and toss to coat with marinade.

VARIATIONS

- Substitute a pound of sea scallops for the shrimp.

- Spice up the dish by adding one-quarter teaspoon of dried red pepper flakes.

- Use chopped, fresh basil instead of parsley.

Mixed Fry
Frito Misto

The Italian phrase "fritto misto" translates as "mixed fry." It can include all sorts of fried foods fish, meats, sweetbreads, vegetables and even desserts.

Serving Fritto Misto di Mare is a special treat for the holidays or special occasions. Our family would serve this platter on Christmas eve. I recommend about 4 pounds of fish, and you can choose from some suggestions listed here:

- Fresh white fish
- Baby squid
- Small crabs
- Shrimp
- Assorted shellfish, tiny whiting or sole.

THE INGREDIENTS

Ingredients for the Batter:
- 1 cup all purpose flour
- 1/2 teaspoon salt
- 1 cup white wine
- 1/4 cup seltzer or club soda

Ingredients for Dredging:
- 1 cup all purpose flour
- 1/2 teaspoon salt
- 1/2 teaspoon black pepper

Ingredients for the Fritto Misto:
- 4 cups sunflower oil
- 1/2 pound medium shrimp, peeled
- 1 pound cleaned squid, cut in 1/2 inch pieces
- 1/2 pound bay scallops
- 1 pound mussels, steamed and shucked
- 1 pound smelts or sardines
- Sea salt
- Pinch of crushed red pepper for garnish, optional
- Chopped parsley for garnish
- Lemon wedges

THE BATTER

- Make the batter: Put the flour and salt in a small bowl and gradually whisk in the wine to obtain a smooth, lump-free mixture. Rest for 30 minutes. Add seltzer just before frying.

THE DREDGING

- Put the seasoned dredging flour in a shallow bowl near the stove. Place the finished batter and an empty plate next to it. Put fish and other ingredients for frying and a paper towel-lined baking sheet nearby. Put oil in a large wide, deep pot and fasten a candy thermometer to the side. Heat oil to 375 degrees

FRYING THE FISH

- Fry the fish: Working in small batches, dip a few pieces of fish, first into the seasoned flour to coat lightly, then into the batter. Put battered pieces on the empty plate. Slip a few pieces into the hot oil and fry for 3 to 4 minutes, until golden. Remove with tongs or a wire spider and drain on the paper towel lined baking sheet. Hold the fried food in a warm oven while frying additional fish. Make sure to regulate the heat below the pan to keep oil at the correct temperature (adding too many pieces to the oil will cause it to cool.) Remove pieces of batter from the oil between batches with a fine-meshed skimmer. Garnish with parsley and lemon wedges. Continue to fry in small batches until all the fish is used.

VEGETABLE ANTIPASTO
SERVES 6

I like to serve this antipasto in several smaller bowls. Serve plenty of bread and grissini to accompany the antipasto as well as good olive oil and lemon wedges. It makes it beautiful and interesting to use a combination of fresh, roasted, and pickled vegetables. This is a good antipasto to serve before a heavier meal.

THE INGREDIENTS

- 12 asparagus spears
- 12 marinated mushrooms
- 12 marinated onions
- 6 arricini (see page 26)
- Selection of olives
- 6 tapenade crostini
- 6 stuffed artichokes (see page 26)
- Lemon wedges
- Extra virgin olive oil

GRILLING

- Grilling or using a barbeque gives the vegetables a more complex and smoky flavor. The marks from the grill look attractive on the platter

OVEN ROASTING

- Oven roasting at a low temperature means the water evaporates out of the food as it cooks. This gives the vegetables a rich, more intensive flavor.

MARINATING

- Marinating means combining food with aromatic ingredients so the food takes on the marinade's flavors. It works particularly well with olives when cracked and mixed with chilies and garlic, citrus and olive oil.

TAPENADE CROSTINI
SERVES 8-10

Crostini are small pieces of bread toasted in the oven, rather than larger broiled slices used for bruschetta.

INGREDIENTS

- 2-day-old ciabatta bread or baguette
- ¼ cup of olive oil
- make the crostini by preheating the oven to 350* F. Be sure to thinly slice the bread and cut each piece in quarters for larger loaves.
- Lightly toast the bread in the oven until crisp.

INSTRUCTIONS

- 2 cups whole black olives, pitted
- 1 ¾ oz. anchovy filets
- 1 tablespoon capers
- 2 garlic cloves, crushed
- ¼ cup basil, finely chopped
- Grated zest and juice of a lemon
- ¾ cup of olive oil

Finely chop the olives, anchovies and capers together with a knife or food processor and put in a bowl. Add the garlic, basil, lemon zest and juice; stir in the olive oil and season well. Serve atop the crostini.

This tapenade will keep in an airtight container in the refrigerator for up to a month with a layer of olive oil on the top.

RED PEPPER CROSTINI

SERVES 6

- 3 Tablespoons extra-virgin olive oil
- 1 onion, finely chopped
- 2 red peppers, thinly sliced
- 2 garlic cloves, crushed
- 1 tablespoon capers, drained and chopped
- 2 tablespoon balsamic vinegar
- 1 tablespoon roughly chopped flat-leaf parsley

Heat the olive oil in a frying pan and cook the onion for a few minutes until soft. Add the peppers and cook for 15 minutes, stirring frequently. Season, then add the garlic and cook for about a minute. Add the capers and vinegar and simmer gently for a few minutes to reduce the liquid. Add the parsley just before spreading on the crostini.

CHICKEN LIVER CROSTINI

SERVES 6

- 7 oz. chicken livers
- 3 tablespoons olive oil
- 1 small onion, finely chopped
- 2 garlic cloves, crushed
- 1 tablespoon finely chopped sage
- 2 tablespoons dry marsala
- 2 tablespoons mascarpone or cream cheese

Instructions

Trim the chicken livers of any sinew. Heat the olive oil in a frying pan and gently cook the onion for 2-3 minutes. Push the onions to the side, increase the heat and add the livers. Cook until they are slightly browned on both sides, then add the garlic and sage and cook for 1 minute. Add the Marsala and cook to reduce the liquid. Season to your liking. Chop to a paste in a food processor or by hand, then add the mascarpone. The chicken livers can be served warm or cold.

BAGNA CAUDA

SERVES 6-8

INGREDIENTS

THE SAUCE:

- 6 large heads of garlic, peeled and thinly sliced
- 10.5 ounces salt-packed anchovies
- Red wine to clean and cover the anchovies
- 21 ounces extra virgin olive oil,
- Butter, optional, to taste.

OPTIONS FOR RAW VEGETABLES

- Sliced red or yellow bell peppers
- Belgian endive
- Radicchio
- Savoy, red, or green cabbage
- Scallions placed in a glass with some Barbera wine
- Radishes
- Carrots
- Celery
- Fennel

OPTIONS FOR COOKED VEGETABLES

- Potatoes, boiled, peeled, and sliced beets, cooked and sliced
- Butternut squash, fried or roasted and sliced onions, roasted whole, then peeled and cut into wedges.
- Bell peppers, roasted and cut into wide strips
- Cauliflower, cooked until tender, yet firm, cut into florets

INSTRUCTIONS

- **Using fresh anchovies:** clean the anchovies, and rinse off the salt. Remove the dorsal fin and carefully open the anchovy like a book. Remove the bones and tail. Place the filets in a dish in a single layer and cover them with red wine. Place the anchovies in the refrigerator until ready to use.

- **Using canned anchovies:** Always use the best quality anchovies in a tin available.

- Once your garlic and anchovies are prepped, you can start cooking the sauce. Add the garlic with about a cup of the oil to your cooking vessel over low heat. Heat slowly and once hot, add the anchovies and the rest of the oil. Cook, stirring occasionally until the anchovies have dissolved and the garlic is tender enough to smash to a cream with a fork or the back of a wooden spoon. This will take about an hour.

- Once the sauce is cooked, you can serve it as is or blend it with an immersion blender if you want a smoother sauce. Add a pat of butter if you wish. Serve the sauce warm with the raw and cooked vegetables. Serve with bread.

OTHER OPTIONAL ACCOMPANIMENTS

- Eggs, hard boiled and cut into wedges
- Bread
- Polenta, sliced and baked until browned

BALSMIC

Crostini with
Balsamic Strawberries and Ricotta

Crostini Balsamic Strawberries and Ricotta

> **Notes:**
> These crostini make the prettiest appetizers to serve at your next picnic, Mother's Day brunch or bridal shower.

Ingredients

- 1 ½ cup strawberries, chopped
- 3/4 cup balsamic vinegar
- 3 tsp. lemon zest
- 4 tsp. brown sugar
- ¾ cup. ricotta
- 1 baguette

- Slice the baguette into ½ inch slices. Toast them at 350 F. for 5 minutes or until nicely toasted. While your tiny toasts are toasting, chop strawberries into teeny, tiny pieces.

- If your strawberries are very ripe, you might want to place them on a paper towel while you prepare the balsamic reduction sauce to allow the juice to release. Otherwise, the strawberry juices will water down the sauce when combined.

Instructions

- In a small saucepan, add balsamic vinegar and brown sugar. Reduce the vinegar over medium heat, stirring occasionally, for 6-8 minutes, until the consistency is somewhat thick and saucy. While the sauce reduces, prepare lemon zest.

- Combine strawberries and lemon zest, pour the balsamic reduction sauce into your measuring cup or bowl, and gently stir. Add a little ricotta to each toast, then carefully add the delicious balsamic strawberries to the crostini. Only use fresh strawberries because frozen strawberries will release too much liquid once thawed and will be a bit too mushy to give these crostini a nice, fresh texture.

- Assemble the crostini about 20 minutes before serving. If you want to prepare your strawberries and sauce a few hours beforehand, simply keep the chopped strawberries and sauce separate until you're ready to assemble the crostini.

LEARNING TECHNIQUES WITH THE Bruschetta

Bruschetta with parma ham, gorgonzola, walnuts, and rocket dressed with balsamic vinegar.

People always ask me about the difference between bruschetta and crostini. Crostini are "little toasts" in Italian, small, thin slices of toasted bread, which are usually brushed with olive oil.

Bruschetta (pronounced broo-skett-ah.) comes from the Latin word bruscare, which simply means "to roast over coals. This traditional garlic bread is made by rubbing slices of toasted bread with garlic cloves, then drizzling the bread with extra-virgin olive oil. The bread is salted and peppered, then heated and served warm. Another difference in serving between these two is that crostini is often served with the bread in a basket and the toppings in bowls for guests to assemble themselves. While bruschetta is served already assembled with the toppings.

WHITE BEAN AND PROSCIUTTO BRUSCHETTA

- 2 cups drained and rinsed cannellini beans
- 1 ¼ teaspoon wine vinegar
- 1 tablespoon extra virgin olive oil
- ¾ teaspoon chopped fresh thyme or ¼ teaspoon of dried thyme
- ½ teaspoon salt
- ⅛ teaspoon black pepper
- 2 ½ teaspoons of fresh parsley
- 2 ounces of thinly sliced prosciutto, cut in strips

INSTRUCTIONS

- Put the beans in a bowl and mash to a coarse puree. Stir in vinegar, oil, pepper, thyme, and salt.

- Put 2-3 slices of prosciutto on each piece of bread, top with beans, and garnish with parsley.

BRUSCHETTA

INGREDIENTS FOR TOMATO BASIL BRUSCHETTA

Serves 4

- 4 ripe tomatoes
- 1 tablespoon basil, shredded
- Roughly chop the tomatoes, and mix them with the basil. Spoon over hot bread and drizzle with olive oil.

INGREDIENTS FOR WILD MUSHROOM BRUSCHETTA

Serves 4

- 2 tablespoons extra virgin olive oil
- 4 ½ cups wild mushrooms
- 2 garlic cloves, crushed
- 1 heaped tablespoon thyme, crushed
- Instructions
- Heat the oil, add the mushrooms, stirring until cooked. Season with salt and pepper. Keep cooking until the liquid is evaporated. Add the garlic and thyme and cook for a minute or two. Spoon over hot bread and serve immediately.

INGREDIENTS FOR EGGPLANT BRUSCHETTA

Serves 4

- 1 medium eggplant
- 1 garlic clove, crushed
- 1/4 cup extra virgin olive oil
- Juice of a small lemon
- 1 tablespoon of roughly chopped mint
- Heat the griddle on the stove and cook eggplant slices over moderately high heat until soft and cooked, turning once. Mix together the garlic, oil, lemon juice, and mint and season well. Put the eggplant in a dish and let it marinate for 30 minutes. Serve on bread and serve at room temperature.

CHICK PEAS

INGREDIENTS

- 1 pound dried chickpeas
- 2 quarts water
- 1 medium white onion, thinly slice
- 1 large carrot, peeled, cut in half
- 1 large celery stalk, cut into thirds
- 4 fat cloves garlic, peeled
- Peel from one lemon, yellow part only
- ¼ cup extra virgin olive oi
- 1 teaspoon baking powder
- 2 teaspoons coarse sea salt

Tip: Allow to cool completely before storing in their broth in the refrigerator for up to one week. Also, the longer your beans have soaked, the shorter the cooking time.

INSTRUCTIONS

- Place the beans in a large bowl and cover by at least 3 inches of water. Stir in the salt. Leave on the counter to soak for 10 hours or up to 24 hours.

- When ready to cook, drain the beans and rinse well. Add them to a large pot, along with all the ingredients listed to cook the beans. Bring the pot to a boil, then cover, reduce heat to the lowest setting and simmer for 1 1/2 to 2 hours or until the beans are tender and mash easily when squashed between your fingers.

- Use them in your hummus or serve as a soup topped with the cooked carrots sliced and some fresh chopped herbs plus a squeeze of lemon.

Mediterranean Hummus

SERVES 6-8

Hummus is a chickpea dip that has its roots in the Middle East. It is a staple in my kitchen and the market at Urbana Farmstead. I make the Mediterranean version most of the time but you can be creative by adding any herb or spice to make your own special treat.

INGREDIENTS

- 3 cups home-cooked chickpeas plus ¼ cup, drained and divided (or use canned)
- ½ cup tahini
- 2 ounces lemon juice (about 1 1/2 lemons)
- 3 cloves garlic, smashed and peeled
- 1/2 teaspoon ground cumin
- 1 cup ice cubes
- extra virgin olive oil, to taste
- 1/4 teaspoon paprika
- 1/4 teaspoon za'atar (preferred), dukkah or ground cumin

INSTRUCTIONS

- Place 3 cups of the drained chickpeas, tahini, lemon juice, garlic and cumin into a blender, preferably a high-powered one. Blend on high until smooth. Add the ice and blend again until smooth, light, and fluffy. Taste and add salt or lemon juice to your preference.

- To serve, spread hummus on a plate, turning the dish to create a swirl. Place reserved 1/4 cup chickpeas in the center. Drizzle olive oil to taste over the hummus. Sprinkle the paprika on one side and the za'atar or spice of preference on the other. Serve with warmed bread or raw vegetables of choice.

- Tip: Store leftovers in the refrigerator. Hummus will be even better the next day. Stir well before serving.

ARANCINI

INGREDIENTS

PREPARE RISOTTO RICE

- 1 1/2 cups arborio rice
- 2 shallots finely chopped
- 1 tsp saffron
- 1/2 cup white wine
- 3 1/4 cups chicken stock good quality
- 2 tbsp Parmesan freshly grated
- 1 tbsp olive oil
- Salt and pepper to season
- Keep the chicken stock warm in a saucepan and get a ladle ready

- Add olive oil to a large pan/skillet on low-medium heat, then add the chopped shallots. Saute the shallots until translucent but not browned.

- Add the rice and stir to coat the grains in the oils, then add the wine. Simmer for 2 minutes, then add 1 ladleful of chicken stock. Let the rice absorb the chicken stock whilst constantly stirring when it's almost absorbed, add another ladle of stock, and continue with the same process.

- When you only have 2 ladlefuls of stock left, add the saffron, then continue until all the stock is gone. As you stir, the saffron will get deeper in color. Season with a generous pinch of salt and add the parmesan.

- Taste for seasoning, then serve.

Additional Information

- Slowly cook the shallots so they don't burn (it'll affect the flavor of the whole dish) and they don't take long! Don't add the saffron too early as it'll start to lose its flavor. You can add more or less saffron to your liking but remember to not add too much as it can be overpowering to most people. The yellow color will deepen as the risotto cooks so wait a few minutes before adding more if you are looking a deep yellow color.

- Use high-quality chicken or vegetable stock. I like to use homemade food when possible. Risotto tends to need a lot more salt than you think so always taste it throughout. Leftovers can be stored in the fridge for 1-2 days or frozen in suitable containers.

PREPARE THE SAUCE

- 2 tablespoons olive oil
- 1 onion, finely chopped
- 1 clove garlic, minced
- 1 1/2 pounds ground meat of veal/beef/pork (any combination you prefer)
- 1/4 cup wine, red or white
- 2 cups tomato passata- tomato purée
- salt and pepper, to taste
- 1 cup frozen peas

For the lega (batter):
- 2 1/2 cup water
- 2 1/3 cup all-purpose flour
- 1 pinch salt

For bread
- 3 2/3 cup breadcrumbs

For frying:
- 3 1/8 quart vegetable oil

INSTRUCTIONS

In a large saucepan, on medium heat sauté the onion and garlic in the olive oil. Add the ground meat and brown, stirring frequently. Add the wine and cook for 1 minute until it evaporates. Pour in the tomato passata and bring to a boil. Lower the heat, cover loosely with the lid and simmer for 1 hour until the sauce has thickened. Add salt and pepper to taste. In the last 10 minutes of cooking, stir in the peas. Set aside to cool.

Prepare the arancini:
- First, have all the necessary ingredients at hand and equip yourself with trays, racks, etc . The preparation of the arancini is a kind of assembly line that becomes more pleasant, or at least less stressful if previously organized.
- Start with the preparation of the lega (batter): This is the batter of water and flour that serves to seal the arancini and to create a base for breading, which will help to give proper browning, thickness, and crunchiness. Pour the water into a deep bowl, add the flour and a nice pinch of salt, and mix well with a whisk. Set aside.

Shape the arancini:
- With one hand, take a little rice according to the size of the arancini you want.
- Shape it into a ball for those to be stuffed with meat and an oval for those with butter.
- Place the future arancini on a tray and continue until the rice is finished.
- Leave them to rest for half an hour so that the rice becomes compact, making the filling process easier. Holding the rice ball with one hand, with the thumb of the other hand, creates a hole in the top center and begins to enlarge it by pushing both downward and to the sides. Place the rice ball back on the tray and move on to the others until all are completed.

ARANCINI

CONTINUATION OF RECIPE

FILL THE ARANCINI:

- Place the chosen filling inside the hole previously created and close the arancina a little by pushing the dressing downwards and trying to bring the rice forward.

- Turn the arancina in your hands to give it its shape and to make the surface smooth and compact, without holes or small cracks.

- Place it on the tray and move on to another, until all are completed.

- At the end, wash your hands and repeat the operation with the second filling.

FRY THE ARANCINI:

- Whisk the batter and immerse each arancina individually, then place them on a wire rack set on a tray.

- Pour the breadcrumbs into a pan and roll each arancina in the breadcrumbs, pressing them well with your hands to ensure the breadcrumbs stick, to compact the surface of the arancine, and if necessary, to regain their shape a little. Pour the oil into a fairly tall saucepan.

- When the oil is hot (about 390°F*), immerse the arancine for 2-3 minutes or until golden. Serve immediately.

MACCU DI FAVE

- **Fresh Fava Beans** remove fava from their pods. Bring a medium size pot of water to a boil; add a little salt and plunge beans into boiling water. Cook for 5 minutes, then using a slotted spoon, transfer into a bowl with cold water. Drain beans, then gently peel; discard skin and set on the side.

- **Dried Fava Beans** rinse the dry fava beans and place in a 6 quart sauce pot with about 4 quarts of water. Soak for 24 hours and change the water at least 2 times. Using a paring knife, eliminate the little dark membrane on top of each bean, remove and discard the bitter outer skin and set on the side.

- 2 cups dried fava beans (1lb.) or 3 cups fresh, removed from their pods 2 whole cloves of garlic ¼ cup of extra virgin olive oil 2 teaspoons of crushed fennel seeds Green foliage of bulb fennel for garnish

- In a 6 quart saucepan, sauté the whole garlic in 2 tablespoons of olive oil over a high heat. Add the fava beans and cover with 2 inches of water. Keep a pot with boiling water on the side to add if the fava becomes too dry. Bring to a boil then simmer covered for 45 minutes stirring occasionally, then add in the crushed fennel seeds. Liquid should be at least 1 inch above the beans at all times. Continue simmering at a very low heat for an additional one and a half hours; keep stirring and adding boiling water if it becomes too dry.

- Cook the Maccu until it has a creamy consistency. Remove from the heat, mix in the remaining extra virgin olive oil and add some salt to taste. Garnish with the foliage of fennels. Serve with crusty bread, crushed red pepper and olive oil.

Fava beans stir so many wonderful memories of my Grandmother Susie. She loved fava beans! My grandfather grew them for her in their little urban backyard. The beginning of Spring meant time with my Nonna shelling, cooking fresh ones, and drying the rest of the crop for the year. My family was poor so they dried vegetables and fruits in the summer on a screen. I love fava beans also.

They bring me tremendous happiness for their taste and fond memories. This fava recipe is a classic Sicilian soup that dates back to Roman times. From the name Macchus, a gluttonous character of Roman comedies. We always ate this soup during the feast of St Joseph, 19th March. Maccu is a recipe with sentiments of renewal– use up the old, and celebrate the new. To make Maccu, the dried beans of the last season are used before the new harvest begins in spring. It is a nutritious and filling starter.

"Insalata Caprese" literally means "the Salad of Capri." This is one of the classic summer dishes in Italy and in the world, especially when garden tomatoes are ripe. A simple platter of garden tomatoes, fresh mozzarella, a swirl of extra virgin olive oil, and a handful of basil leaves makes the perfect first course to any meal.

INSALATA CAPRESE

INGREDIENTS

- 3 to 4 medium ripe tomatoes (about 1 1/2 pounds), sliced ¼ inch thick
- 1 pound fresh mozzarella cheese, sliced into ¼ inch thick rounds
- 1/2 cup packed fresh basil leaves
- Flaky sea salt
- Freshly ground black pepper
- 2 tablespoons extra-virgin olive oil
- 2 tablespoons balsamic glaze

- Place the tomatoes and mozzarella on a platter. Arrange tomatoes and mozzarella on a platter in an alternating pattern. Top with the basil leaves. Scatter the basil leaves over the tomatoes and mozzarella.

- Sprinkle with a generous pinch of flaky salt and several grinds of black pepper to taste. Drizzle the olive oil and balsamic glaze over the tomatoes, mozzarella and basil. Serve immediately.

- **Option**: Using pesto to garnish creates a beautiful presentation and it is delicious with the tomatoes and mozzarella.

- **Tip**: Make your own Balsamic Vinegar Glaze. Great for drizzling over caprese salads, grilled veggies and proteins - and even vanilla ice cream.

BALSAMIC VINEGAR GLAZE

- 2 cups balsamic vinegar

- Pour the vinegar into a small saucepan and bring to a boil over medium-high heat. Reduce the heat to medium and simmer, occasionally stirring, until the vinegar thickens, coats the back of a spoon, and is reduced to about 1/2 cup, 20 to 25 minutes. Set aside to cool for 10 minutes; the glaze will thicken slightly as it cools.

- **Tip for Storage:** Balsamic glaze can be stored in an airtight container in the refrigerator for up to one month.

CAPRESE SALAD WITH BURRATA

INGREDIENTS

- 8 oz mixed cherry tomatoes, halved
- Burrata - 8 oz room temperature
- 5 basil leaves, cut into ribbons
- Extra virgin olive oil
- Sea salt and black pepper
- 1 loaf artisan bread, sliced
- 1 garlic clove, skin removed

INSTRUCTIONS

- Grill or toast the bread and rub each piece with garlic and add a drizzle of extra virgin olive oil. Layer the tomatoes on a plate, arrange the burrata in the middle and scatter basil ribbons on top. Add a swirl of extra virgin olive, a sprinkle of sea salt and a few cracks of black pepper.

Serve with the grilled or toasted bread.

THE STORY
Behind My Recipe

Like so many other dishes throughout Italy, the ingredients in Minestrone Soup are defined by each region. Rooted in seasonal produce with a few fixed elements, such as beans, vegetables, and some form of pasta, rice or other grains. It is a simple but hearty soup served before a meal or as the meal. It is also a soup for all seasons, as good in autumn and winter as in spring and summer.

In Liguria, you'll find it laced with pesto and plenty of grated parmesan. The family I stayed with in Sardinia called Minestrone Soup, their longevity soup, because it is a full dose of daily vegetables and beans. Our family recipe, Minestrone alla Napoletana, adds eggplant. I have two recipes to share. One I make all the time and sell in the market at Urbana Farmstead and the other I serve in the winter when a heartier soup is needed. This summer minestrone soup is loaded with seasonal vegetables like zucchini, corn, tomatoes, and green beans. With plenty of fresh herbs and two types of beans for fiber and protein, it's filling, flavorful, and super easy to make in just 30 minutes!

This summer minestrone soup is loaded with seasonal vegetables like zucchini, corn, tomatoes, and green beans. With plenty of fresh herbs and two types of beans for fiber and protein, it's filling, flavorful, and super easy to make in just 30 minutes!

Campania, Italy

Sardinia, Italy

Mangiamo | 32

SUMMER MINESTRONE

SERVES 6-8

INGREDIENTS

- 1/4 cup butter
- 1 yellow onion, diced (1 1/2 cups)
- 4 cloves of garlic, finely minced
- 1 1/2 cups thinly sliced celery
- 1 cup diced zucchini
- 1 cup green beans, sliced into 1" pieces
- 1 medium bell pepper, diced
- 1 1/2 cup frozen baby lima beans or purple hull peas
- 3/4 cup fresh or frozen corn
- 1 14.5 oz can diced tomatoes
- 3 cups chopped swiss chard or spinach
- 1/3 cup flat leaf parsley, finely chopped
- 1/4 cup finely chopped fresh basil (or 4 tsp dried)
- 2 tbsp finely chopped fresh thyme (or 2 tsp dried)
- 6 cups vegetable broth
- 2 tbsp tomato paste
- 1 1/2 tbsp white wine vinegar
- 1 can navy beans, drained and rinsed
- 1 tsp fine grain kosher salt
- 1/2 tsp ground black pepper

INSTRUCTIONS

- Heat butter in a large soup pot over medium. Add onions, garlic, and celery. Sauté, stirring occasionally, for 5-7 minutes. Add zucchini, green beans, bell pepper, lima beans, corn, tomatoes, tomato paste, salt and pepper. Stir well and continue cooking for 5 minutes. Add in broth and white wine vinegar and bring to a boil. Once boiling, add chopped greens, parsley, basil, and thyme. Stir well, cover, and reduce heat to low.

- Simmer for 15 minutes, then add in navy beans and cook for an additional 10-15 minutes. Serve with more fresh basil and vegan parmesan.

- **Tip for storage:** Let soup cool to room temperature, then transfer to an airtight container and refrigerate for 5 days. Reheat in a small pot over medium heat.

- **Tip for freezer storage:** Let the soup cool completely before transferring to an airtight, freezer-safe container. Freeze for up to 6 months. To reheat, defrost in the refrigerator overnight, then heat over medium heat in a pot.

- **Beans:** I prefer cannellini beans, but you can also use navy beans, Great Northern, garbanzo, or pinto beans.
- **Lima beans:** I like lima beans, so I add frozen ones. If you prefer, substitute frozen peas or shelled edamame.
- **Greens:** Swiss chard is my first choice, but I also use spinach or kale.
- **Tomatoes:** if you'd prefer not to use canned or have some extra fresh tomatoes on hand, sub the can with 3-4 finely diced roma tomatoes.
- **Corn:** I add fresh sweet corn in season, but you can also substitute frozen. Fire-roasted corn is also a great choice!

SUMMER MINESTRONE

WINTER MINESTRONE

SOUPS

CLASSIC LENTIL

SPLIT PEA

WINTER MINESTRONE

SERVES 6-8

This version has more beans and a grain for cold winter nights.

INGREDIENTS

- ½ cup dried peeled fava beans
- ½ cup dried cranberry beans
- ⅓ cup dried chickpeas
- 7 tablespoons extra-virgin olive oil
- 1 medium yellow onion, chopped (about 1 cup)
- 2 medium carrots, peeled and chopped (about ⅔ cup)
- 2 medium celery stalks, chopped (about ½ cup)
- Add other fresh vegetables from the garden if you would like, such as zucchini, cabbage, green beans, cauliflower or broccoli florets
- 2 teaspoons minced garlic
- 1 28-ounce can of crushed tomatoes (about 3½ cups)
- 3 medium yellow potatoes, peeled and diced (about 1½ cups)
- 1 ½ cups chopped fennel fronds and bulbs
- ¼ cup loosely packed fresh Italian flat-leaf parsley leaves, chopped 2 tablespoons chopped fresh basil leaves
- ⅔ cup of a small pasta or fregola, small pasta or couscous
- ½ teaspoon salt
- ½ teaspoon freshly ground black pepper
- ¼ cup finely grated Pecorino Romano (about 2 ounces)

INSTRUCTIONS

- Soak the fava beans, cranberry beans and chickpeas in a large bowl of water overnight. Drain in a colander set in the sink. Rinse well.

- Warm 3 tablespoons of the olive oil in a large soup pot or Dutch oven set over medium high heat. Add the onion, carrots, and celery; cook, stirring often, until soft but not browned, about 5 minutes. Add the garlic and cook until fragrant, about 20 seconds.

- Stir in the tomatoes, potatoes, fennel, parsley, and basil, as well as the drained beans and chickpeas. Add enough water (6 to 8 cups) so that everything is submerged by 1 inch. Raise the heat to high and bring to a full boil. Reduce the heat to low and simmer slowly, uncovered, until the beans are tender, adding more water as necessary; if the mixture gets too thick, about 1 ½ hours.

- Stir in the pasta, salt and pepper. Add up to 2 cups of water if the soup seems too dry. Continue simmering, uncovered, until the pasta is tender, about 10 minutes. Drizzle with extra virgin olive oil and grated cheese.

Tip: Add a teaspoon of fennel seeds to the aromatic vegetables you sauté to begin the dish.

CLASSIC LENTIL SOUP

SERVES 6-8

INGREDIENTS

- 2 tablespoons olive oil
- 1 medium onion, diced
- 2 medium celery stalks, diced
- 2 medium carrots, diced
- 4 garlic cloves, minced
- 6 cups low sodium vegetable broth
- 2 cups dried brown lentils
- 1 teaspoon dried rosemary (or 1 tablespoon fresh)
- 2 teaspoons dried thyme leaves (or 2 tablespoons fresh)
- 1/2 teaspoon black pepper
- 1 bay leaf
- 1 (14 ounce or 400 ml) can diced tomatoes
- 2 teaspoons red wine vinegar
- Salt to taste

INSTRUCTIONS

- Coat the bottom of a large pot with the oil and place it over medium heat. Once the oil is hot, add the onion, carrots and celery. Sweat the veggies for about 5 minutes, stirring often, until they begin to soften up. Add the garlic and cook it with the veggies for about 1 minute, until very fragrant.

- Stir in the broth, lentils, rosemary, thyme, black pepper, and bay leaf. Raise the heat and bring the liquid to a boil. Lower the heat and allow the soup to simmer for about 25 minutes, stirring occasionally, until the lentils are almost fully cooked but just a bit on the firm side. You can add water while the soup simmers if it becomes too dry.

- Stir in the tomatoes and let the soup continue simmering for 5 to 10 minutes, until the lentils are tender. Remove the pot from heat and remove the bay leaf. Stir in the vinegar and season the soup with salt to taste. Ladle into bowls and serve.

SPLIT PEA SOUP

SERVES 6-8

This version has more beans and a grain for cold winter nights.

INGREDIENTS

- 2 Tablespoons butter
- 1 small onion chopped
- 3 large carrots diced
- 3 celery stalks diced
- 3 cloves garlic minced
- 1 pound dried split peas
- 6 cups chicken broth more if needed
- 1 1/2 - 2 pound ham bone
- 1/2 teaspoon salt
- 1/4 teaspoon pepper
- 1 teaspoon fresh thyme
- 1 cup chopped ham for garnish

INSTRUCTIONS

- In a large pot over medium-high heat add the butter and let it melt. Add the onion, carrots, celery, and garlic. Sauté until tender.

- Add in the split peas and chicken broth. Add in the ham bone. Bring to a boil and simmer uncovered for 60-90 minutes stirring occasionally. Cook until the peas split and the soup has thickened.

- Remove the ham bone and shred the ham. Add it back to the soup. Add salt, pepper, and thyme. Garnish with additional ham if needed.

SHOPPING List

Every Italian child waits to grow tall enough to work at a table with nonna and make pasta! I was no exception. I learned from my Bisnonna, Vincenza. And made pasta many times with my Nonna Susie, my Mother and cousins. I taught both of my girls and grandchildren to make pasta.

The real challenge in making fresh pasta is learning to trust your hands. Feeling food is something my nonna and mother taught me. My mom would say, 'Just feel it!' when I ask if I got her recipe right. It's good to learn to trust your instincts, and using your hands helps. This is especially important in pasta making because it is difficult to measure ingredients exactly. Variable egg sizes and moisture content of the flour can affect how much of each you actually need.

PASTA E GNOCCHI

Campania, Italy

Sicily, Italy

LEARNING
TECHNIQUE
MAKING EGG PASTA DOUGH

Fresh egg pasta is made from eggs and flour. This recipe makes a soft pliable pasta that can be easily shaped into a homemade pasta like lasagna, ravioli, tagliatelle, or tortellini.

- 3 cups 00 or all-purpose flour
- 2 large eggs
- 4-6 egg yolks, plus more as needed
- 1 ¼ cups fine semolina flour

Mound the flour in the center of a large, wide mixing bowl or on a marble counter. Dig a well in the center of the mound and add eggs and yolks. Using a fork, beat together the eggs and begin to incorporate the flour, starting with the inner rim of the well. The dough will start to come together in a shaggy mass when about half of the flour is incorporated. Use your fingers to continue to mix the dough. Press any loose bits of flour into the mass of dough. If needed, add another egg yolk to absorb all of the flour until the dough comes together into a cohesive mass.

Transfer to a lightly floured surface and knead by hand for 5 to 8 more minutes until the dough is smooth, elastic and uniform in color. The dough should not stick to your finger if pressed in the middle. If it does stick, add more flour and continue to knead. Wrap the dough in plastic and set aside for at least 30 minutes (and up to 4 hours) at room temperature.

LEARNING TECHNIQUE WITH Dough

- **ROLLING OUT FRESH PASTA DOUGH**

Divide the dough into six to eight flattened rectangular pieces and cover with saran wrap to prevent drying out. Dust the surface with semolina (flour will make the pasta harder). Using a rolling pin, flatten the first piece so it fits into the pasta machine roller. Feed the pasta through the rollers on the widest setting. Fold the flattened pasta in half or thirds to fit across the roller. Repeat three times. If you are not using a machine, continue to use your rolling pin.

- **CUTTING PAST BY MACHINE**

Attach the cutting blades to your machine, wide for tagliatelle and narrow for linguine. Feed a sheet of pasta into the machine and carefully collect the cut pasta as it comes out the other end. Hang it up immediately or coil into wide nests. To keep the nests from sticking, toss them with a little more semolina.

- **CUTTING BY HAND**

Roll out the pasta into long flat sheets and dust them with semolina to prevent cut noodles from sticking. Roll up each sheet loosely and cut into slices of whatever width you want. The thicker widths are easier to handle when they are rolled. Hang it up immediately or coil into wide nests. To keep the nests from sticking, toss them with a little more semolina.

RICOTTA GNOCCHI

SERVES 4

INGREDIENTS

- 1 1/2 cups (one 15-ounce container) whole milk ricotta cheese
- 3 egg yolks
- 1 cup (about 4 ounces) '00' flour or all-purpose flour
- 3/4 cup (about 1 ounce) freshly-grated Parmesan
- 3/4 teaspoon fine sea salt
- 1/4 teaspoon freshly-cracked black pepper

INSTRUCTIONS

- Prep the water: Bring a large stockpot of generously-salted water to a boil over high heat.

- Drain the ricotta: While your water is heating, place 3-4 paper towels on a large plate and spread the ricotta on the paper towels in an even layer. Place another layer of 3-4 paper towels on top of the ricotta. Then press down gently to let the excess moisture soak into the paper towels, trying to soak up as much of the excess liquid as possible. Transfer the ricotta to a large mixing bowl. (If it sticks to the paper towels, just use a rubber spatula to scrape it off.) The drained ricotta should now weigh about 12 ounces.

- Mix your dough ingredients. Add the egg yolks to the ricotta and stir briefly to combine. Add in the flour, Parmesan, salt and pepper, and stir until evenly combined. Avoid over-mixing. The dough will be a bit moist and maybe sticky, but it should hold together well. If it feels too wet, just add another few tablespoons of flour.

- Roll out and cut the dough. Shape the dough into a round disk with your hands, then transfer it to a lightly-floured cutting board and sprinkle the dough lightly with flour. Using a knife or a bench scraper, cut the dough into eight even pie wedges.

- Using your hands, gently roll each wedge out into an even log, approximately 3/4-inch wide. Cut each log into individual bite-sized little gnocchi squares. Lightly dust the gnocchi with flour once more and give them a quick toss so that they are all lightly coated with flour. (This will help prevent them from sticking together.)

- Boil the gnocchi. Carefully transfer the gnocchi to the boiling water to cook. Then once they float — usually after 30 seconds or so — drain the gnocchi. Serve immediately, tossed with your favorite sauce.

SPINACH RICOTTA GNOCCHI

SERVES 4

INGREDIENTS

FOR THE GNOCCHI

- 15 oz. whole milk ricotta cheese
- 1 cup semolina flour
- 3 large egg yolks
- 10 oz. frozen (thawed) or fresh spinach, drained
- ¾ cup finely grated Parmesan cheese plus more for serving
- ½ tsp kosher salt
- ¼ tsp black pepper

INSTRUCTIONS

- Using several paper towels, squeeze the excess liquid from the spinach. Using a medium mixing bowl, add all gnocchi ingredients and stir until well combined. Cover bowl with plastic wrap and let rest for ~30 minutes. While the dough is resting, bring a large pot of salted water to a boil.

- Roll dough into a log approximately 1" thick. Slice log into ~1" pieces.m Add gnocchi to boiling water; cook until gnocchi floats (~1-2 minutes). Using a slotted spoon, transfer the cooked gnocchi into a large bowl.

- To serve, add sauce to plates and top with gnocchi. Before serving, drizzle the top of the dish with olive oil and sprinkle with Parmesan cheese and freshly chopped Italian parsley.

THE STORY
Behind My Recipe

Now it is time to make the sauces. First let me say that the term "Gravy" doesn't exist in Italy. So you won't be hearing me call anything that goes over pasta "gravy."

Thinking about sauces brings me right back to my childhood. I have so many memories involving food, but thinking about noon, after Sunday mass, when the family congregated at my Nonno Marty and Nonna Susies' house in South Gate, California, makes my heart flutter with joy. A big part of Sunday dinner was the wonderful food that was prepared each Sunday, some dishes starting early in the morning or the night before. My nonna would get her pots out and start cooking before mass. When we pulled up to her house, you would smell the aroma of the sauce as soon as you got out of the car. Our family Sunday menu was typically pasta and meat, which usually consisted of meatballs, sausages, beef, and pork (including brasciolla). We didn't eat meat every day of the week but Sunday was the day the meat would always be fresh and prepared to perfection. Of course, there was bread, simple dishes with fresh vegetables, sfingi, and a salad to end the meal. My Nonno was a winemaker so we enjoyed his wine with the meal. Then after the cleanup was over, we would have desserts. My passion for food and cooking and most of my culinary memories lead me back to family dinners.

There is nothing better with pasta than a simple red sauce. The two main red sauces are Marinara and Sugo di Pomodoro. The difference mainly comes down to the length of time each pot of sauce spends on the stovetop, simmering to delicious goodness. Originating in Naples, marinara ("sailor-style" because mare means sea) is a classic Italian Sugo (tomato-based sauce). Since Marinara spends less time simmering with chopped larger chunks of tomatoes and sometimes capers are added. It is often served with seafood. Sugo di Pomodoro is simmered longer with minced tomatoes, creating a deep, dark redness closer to burgundy and a smoother and thicker consistency.

Mangiamo | 44

AGLIO, OLIO E PEPERONCINO

RECIPE

Translated into "garlic, oil and chili pepper" it is one of the simplest and most essential Napolitano pasta sauces. Typically served with spaghetti and finely chopped parsley to garnish – no cheese needed. Starchy pasta water is used to help emulsify and thicken the sauce.

- 1 pound dried spaghetti
- Salt (enough to season your pasta water)
- 1 cup extra virgin olive oil
- 6 cloves of garlic, sliced thinly (about 1 clove per person, without the germ)
- Sliced and seeded fresh red chili peppers to taste (or 1 teaspoon crushed red pepper flakes if you don't have fresh ones)
- ½ cup reserved pasta water
- ½ cup chopped parsley
- 4 filets of anchovies (optional)

SPAGHETTI AGLIO, OLIO E PEPERONCINO

- In a medium pot bring water to a boil. Once boiling, add salt to taste (it should taste almost as salty as the sea). Add the pasta and cook it for 1 minute less than the suggested cooking time.

- While the pasta is cooking add half of the olive oil and garlic to a large sauté pan. On medium heat, cook the garlic until it gets very fragrant and translucent (making sure not to burn it). Add the crushed red chili flakes to the pan and let them cook for 1 minute, then add a generous spoonful of pasta water.

- When al dente, strain the pasta and add it to the sauté pan right away. Cook for another minute in the pan, then add the parsley and the rest of the extra virgin olive oil and give it a nice toss in the pan until everything is incorporated. The water sauce will be whipped with the extra virgin olive to create a perfect emulsion of oil, water, and starch

MARINARA SAUCE
SERVES 2

INGREDIENTS

- 2 tablespoons olive oil extra virgin
- 3 cloves garlic crushed and coarsely chopped
- Pinch crushed red pepper flakes optional
- Fresh whole tomatoes or 28-ounce whole canned tomatoes
- 2 sprigs fresh basil
- Salt and pepper to taste
- Garnish with fresh rosemary.

INSTRUCTIONS

- In a large skillet, heat the oil over medium heat. Add the lightly crushed garlic cloves and continue to cook for another minute or so. At this point the garlic should be fragrant. (Make sure not to overcook the garlic as this will produce a bitter sauce)
- If you use fresh tomatoes, blanch 2 lbs of tomatoes and remove the skin. Otherwise, add the tin tomatoes. You can use a potato masher or the back of a wooden spoon to break them up as they are simmering.
- Bring to a boil and then reduce heat to obtain a vigorous simmer. Simmer for about 15-20 minutes or until the sauce is thickened. Add the basil and remove from heat. You can add capers if you want to serve as a side with calamari or shrimp. Garnish with fresh rosemary

SUGO DI POMORDORO
SERVES 6

INGREDIENTS

- 2.5 lbs fresh tomatoes (I use roma tomatoes)
- 1/2 cup olive oil
- 1 small onion, chopped
- 1/2 clove garlic, chopped
- 1/2 small carrot thinly shredded
- 3 basil leaves (if in season) chopped or whole
- Salt and pepper to taste

INSTRUCTION

- Chop the onion. Gently rinse the basil leaves and delicately pat them dry. Wash and dry the tomatoes and remove the eye from each tomato. Using a paring knife, score a cross on the bottom of each tomato.

- Take a large pan full of water, bring the water to the boil, plunge the tomatoes into the pan and blanch for 15-20 seconds until you see some cracks on the tomato skin.

- Using a slotted spoon, remove the tomatoes from the pan. Put the tomatoes into a colander. Peel the tomatoes. Quarter the tomatoes. Remove the core and seeds from each tomato quarter.

- Put the olive oil into a saucepan. Heat the oil and then add the onion. Sweat the onion for 3-4 minutes. Add the diced tomato into the pan. Stir for a few seconds. Cover the pan with a lid, bring the heat to low and let cook for 10 minutes. Give it a good stir and simmer on a very gentle heat for 30 minutes, uncovered, until it thickens. 10 minutes before the finish, taste the sauce and season with salt according to taste. Right before serving, add the basil leaves and a dash of olive oil.

MEAT SAUCES

Most people think of Ragu as a tomato sauce, but it's actually a meat-based (veal, beef, lamb, pork, fish or poultry) sauce with a small amount of tomato sauce added to it. Ragu sauce has more meat and minced elements, specifically minced carrot, celery, and pancetta…also known as soffritto, and is made with wine, beef broth, and usually a little bit of heavy cream or milk poured in it to lighten the color and enrich the flavor. Ragu Alla Bolognese is a variation of Ragu.

Classic Ragù Alla Bolognese, the recipe in the following pages is one of my absolute favorite pasta recipes and it leads me to a special memory of my Nonna Susie. Years after my Nonna Marty died, my nonna visited me in San Diego for a few weeks. Traveling from the airport to my home, my nonna started to scream, "Stop Margaret, Stop, Finocchi! Let's get the finocchi!" I pulled over to figure out why she was so animated and there, in the hills along the highway, she spotted wild fennel. And yes, of course I found a safe place to park before we picked our finocchi!

SUGO ALLA PUTTANESCA

INGREDIENTS

- 10 ounces spaghetti or other long, thin pasta
- 2 tablespoons extra-virgin olive oil
- 3 cloves garlic thinly sliced
- 4 anchovy filets finely chopped
- ¼ teaspoon red pepper flakes or more to taste
- 14 ½ ounces crushed tomatoes with juice
- ½ teaspoon dried oregano
- ½ cup pitted black olives oil cured or kalamata, halved
- 1 tablespoon capers chopped if large
- chopped fresh parsley for garnish

INSTRUCTIONS

- Heat olive oil in a large skillet over medium heat until hot. Add sliced garlic cloves, chopped anchovy filets, and red pepper flakes; cook and stir until mixture is fragrant, about 1 minute. Add tomatoes with juice and oregano; bring to boil. Reduce and simmer for 5 minutes. Stir in olives and capers; simmer 3-5 minutes more, stirring occasionally until thickened.

- In the meantime, cook pasta according to package directions in a large pot of water until al dente. Drain, reserving 1 cup or more of the cooking water. (Ideally, pasta will finish at the same time as the sauce. Stir cooked spaghetti into pasta sauce to coat, adding reserved pasta water as necessary to loosen sauce. Serve garnished with chopped parsley

CLASSIC RAGÙ ALLA BOLOGNESE

SERVES 4

The key ingredient is patience. This recipe begins with cutting your meat and vegetables evenly, then browning your meat and allowing your stock and wine to reduce gently, while you carefully monitor the pot to make sure nothing scorches.

INGREDIENTS

- ⅓ cup dried porcini mushrooms
- 4 tablespoons extra-virgin olive oil
- 4 ounces pancetta, finely diced (about ¾ cup)
- 1 medium yellow onion, finely diced (about 1 cup)
- 1 medium carrot, peeled, finely diced (about ½ cup)
- 1 rib celery, finely diced (about ½ cup)
- Kosher salt, to taste
- 1½ pounds skirt steak, patted dry and cut into ¼-inch cubes
- 4 ounces lean pork shoulder, ground
- 4 sage leaves

INSTRUCTIONS

- Place the porcini in a bowl and cover with ½ cup of boiling water. Allow to sit for 15 minutes to rehydrate. Remove the porcini, reserving the water and finely chop. Set both the chopped mushrooms and the liquid aside.

- In a large, heavy-bottomed pot over medium heat, add 2 tablespoons of the olive oil. Add the pancetta and cook, stirring until the fat begins to render out, 3 to 4 minutes. Add the vegetables and season with salt. Cook, stirring often, until the vegetables begin to soften, 6 to 8 minutes. Add the mushrooms and continue to cook until all of the vegetables are very soft and all the liquid has evaporated, 10 to 12 minutes. Transfer the mixture to a bowl and set aside.

- Return the pot to the stove over medium-high heat and heat the remaining 2 tablespoons of olive oil. Working in 2 batches, brown the skirt steak, 4 to 5 minutes for each batch. Remove the beef using a slotted spoon and transfer to a plate. Add the ground pork to the pot, and using a wooden spoon, break the pork into small clumps. Season it with salt and brown, 2 to 3 minutes. Place the sage, bay leaves and thyme in the center of a triple layer of cheesecloth. Gather up the edges and tie using kitchen twine to form a bouquet garni.

- Reduce the heat to medium and return the browned beef and reserved vegetable mixture to the pot with the bouquet garni and cook, stirring often, until most of the liquid has evaporated, 4 to 5 minutes. Deglaze the pan by adding the wine. Scrape the brown bits on the bottom of the pan using a wooden spoon. Reduce until all the liquid has evaporated and the contents have taken on a rich chestnut color, 10 to 12 minutes.

- Reduce the heat to medium and return the browned beef and reserved vegetable mixture to the pot with the bouquet garni and cook, stirring often, until most of the liquid has evaporated, 4 to 5 minutes. Deglaze the pan by adding the wine. Scrape the brown bits on the bottom of the pan using a wooden spoon. Reduce until all the liquid has evaporated and the contents have taken on a rich chestnut color, 10 to 12 minutes.

- Add the tomato paste and cook for 3 to 4 minutes. Add 1½ cups of the stock and ½ cup of the milk and reduce by half, 12 to 15 minutes. Add the Parmesan rinds, nutmeg and remaining stock and milk, skimming any fat that rises to the surface, and continue cooking until the flavors have come together and the sauce has become very thick, 35 to 45 minutes. Season with salt and allow to cool. Remove and discard the bouquet garni.

- Bolognese is traditionally served with a wider pasta like pappardelle or tagliatelle.such as tagliatelle not spaghetti. Top with fresh-grated Parmigiano Reggiano before serving.

SICILIAN PASTA WITH SARDINES AND WILD FENNEL

Is called 'pasta con le sarde' in Italian and 'pasta ch'i sardi' iin the Sicilian dialect. Sicilian pasta with sardines and wild fennel is a delicious fusion of ingredients from Arab and Mediterranean cultures. In some parts of the island, they add tomatoes or almonds. In other parts, they don't use saffron or tomatoes. But, in general, the recipe calls for fresh sardines, anchovies, sultanas/raisins, pine nuts, saffron, and wild fennel.

INGREDIENTS

- 14 oz pasta or spaghetti
- 14 oz fresh sardines or canned
- 2-3 anchovy filets
- 2-3 bunches wild fennel or fennel tops and fennel seeds
- 1 onion peeled and finely chopped
- 3-4 tbsp extra virgin olive oil
- 1 tsp saffron threads or powder
- 2 oz raisins
- 1 oz pine nuts
- salt for pasta and to taste
- ground black pepper to taste

INSTRUCTIONS

- First, soak the raisins in a bowl of warm water. Then soak the saffron in a small cup along with 3-4 tbsp warm water. Wild fennel is very easy to find in the countryside but if you don't have wild fennel, use the greenest and most tender parts of fennel tops. Remove the lower part of the wild fennel stalks and cook in boiling salted water for 10 minutes. Save the water and drain the fennel and put it into a bowl of iced water to preserve the color.

- If you have fresh sardines, rinse them thoroughly and eliminate the scales by rubbing the body under running water. Open the stomach and discard the entrails. Finally, pull firmly and gently on the head to separate the meat from the backbone. Rinse the fish filets again, dry them, and place in the fridge until ready to cook.

- Put a pot of water onto a boil for the pasta. You can add the fennel water to it. Add salt once it starts to boil (less salt if using the fennel water) and bring to the boil again.

- Peel and chop the onion finely. Drain the fennel and chop it. Then put the onion in a frying pan or skillet with 3 tbsp of olive oil and the anchovy filets. Sautè over a medium heat until the onions are translucent and the anchovies have melted.

- Rinse the raisins and add to the pan along with the pine nuts, saffron and the minced fennel. Cook 5 minutes more, then add the sardine filets. Sautè 3-4 minutes stirring until the fish starts to fall apart. Do not overcook the fish.

- Finally, add salt as needed and another splash of olive oil. Cook the pasta al dente according to the instructions on the packet. Drain and mix with the sardine sauce.
- Serve immediately with toasted breadcrumbs if required.

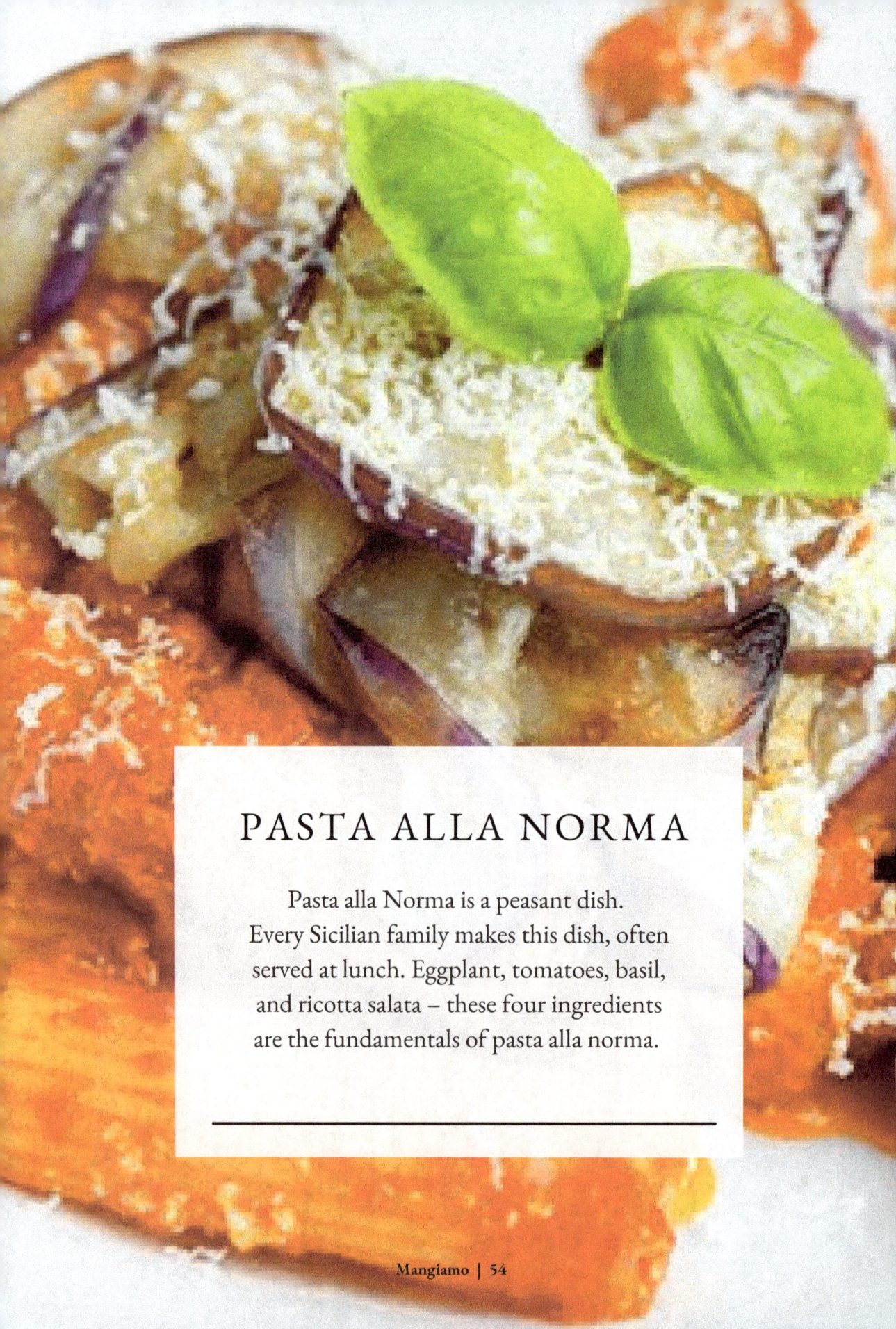

PASTA ALLA NORMA

Pasta alla Norma is a peasant dish. Every Sicilian family makes this dish, often served at lunch. Eggplant, tomatoes, basil, and ricotta salata – these four ingredients are the fundamentals of pasta alla norma.

PASTA ALLA NORMA

SERVES 6

INGREDIENTS

- 1 large (1 to 1 1/2 lbs) eggplant
- Sea salt
- 2 or 3 large (at least 18 oz) ripe tomatoes
- 1/4 cup extra-virgin olive oil plus more for tossing the eggplant
- 1 pound rigatoni or fettuccine
- 2 garlic cloves very thinly sliced
- Crushed red pepper flakes
- 1 bunch basil leaves only, very roughly chopped (about 1 packed cup)
- About 2 tablespoons chopped mint leaves
- About 2 tablespoons chopped flat-leaf parsley leaves
- 1 scant cup ricotta salata crumbled or coarsely grated, optional
- Parmesan cheese optional

INSTRUCTIONS

- Heat the oven to 425°F. Using a vegetable peeler or a paring knife, peel all or some of the skin from the eggplant in stripes (it can be nice to have some, but not all, of the eggplant skin in the final pasta dish). Cut the eggplant into 1-inch dice and toss it on a rimmed baking sheet with enough olive oil to lightly coat it. Sprinkle it with salt.

- Roast the eggplant until browned and very tender, about 20 minutes. The eggplant is done when you can easily squish a cube with your finger and it has a nice, creamy texture.

- Meanwhile, bring a big pot of salted water to a boil. Add the pasta and cook, stirring frequently, according to the package instructions.

- Warm a large skillet over low heat and add the 4 tablespoons of olive oil. Toss in the garlic and crushed red pepper and stir a bit. Add the basil and a sprinkle of salt, raise the heat to medium, and cook, stirring, until the basil is dark green and wilted, being careful not to burn the garlic.
- Add the tomatoes, sprinkle with the salt (if you haven't already), and cook until the tomatoes barely lose their rawness, about 5 minutes. Add the roasted eggplant and let the sauce simmer gently until the pasta is ready.
- Drain the pasta, reserving about 1 cup pasta cooking water. Toss the drained pasta with the sauce, the mint, and the parsley, tasting and adjusting the seasoning if necessary. If the mixture seems dry, add some of the pasta cooking water, a little at a time, until the sauce is your desired consistency. Toss in the ricotta salata, if using, and pass the Parmesan to grate.

LASAGNA DI CARNEVALE

ONE LARGE LASAGNA IS, ENOUGH TO FEED A CROWD

Lasagne di carnevale is a traditional Italian lasagna dish from Naples that is made with a combination of lasagne pasta, sugo, olive oil, salsiccia sausage, white wine, stale bread, ground pork, grated Parmigiano-Reggiano, ricotta, mozzarella, eggs, parsley, salt, and pepper. This kind of dish is perfect for inviting friends and family together to help you make the dish while you eat, drink, laugh and create memories.

FOR TOPPING:
Freshly grated parmesan cheese olive oil

- One batch of sugo (See page 57)
- One batch of fresh egg pasta rolled into lasagna sheets (or 2 boxes of factory-made hard durum wheat lasagna sheets)
- One batch of polpettine (little meatballs) (See page 57)
- 3 or 4 Italian sausages (not spicy) (optional)
- Spring peas
- 1 large ball of mozzarella

THE RICOTTA CREAM:

- 8 oz ricotta cheese
- 3-4 eggs
- 3-1/2 oz freshly grated Parmesan cheese
- A sprig or two of fresh parsley, finely minced
- Salt and pepper

COOKING INSTRUCTIONS

1. MAKE THE SUGO

This step should be done the day before, both because the sugo itself takes several hours to cook and it needs to be cooled and because it tastes much better the next day. Make sure that it is not too thick—loose enough to pour easily—to account for evaporation as the dish bakes. Dilute with water if need be.

2. MAKE THE PASTA

While lasagna di carnevale can be made with factory-made hard durum wheat lasagna, it is so easy to make the dough and roll out the sheets using setting '4' on most pasta machines.

3. MAKE THE POLPETTINE

The lasagna is stuffed with, among other things, polpettine, or little tiny meatballs. The meatballs are small, no more than 1 inch round. Shallow fry them in light olive oil until just golden brown.

4. FRY THE SAUSAGE

In a classic lasagna di carnevale, the stuffing also includes long, thin sausages called cervellatine. In America you can buy them online from Urbana Farmstead at www.urbanafarmstead.net. You can either omit them and just use 'sweet' Italian sausages and fry them in olive oil.

INGREDIENTS

Make the ricotta cream and cut up the mozzarella.
Mix all the ricotta cream ingredients well in a mixing bowl with a spatula.

INSTRUCTIONS

COOK THE PASTA SHEETS:

- Cook the lasagna sheets al dente, remembering that they will cook again in the oven. Since these sheets are thicker than the usual pasta and contain a bit of semolina, however, you will need to cook them for longer than other types of fresh pasta, say around 3-5 minutes, depending on how long they have been left to dry.

- If using factory-made pasta, follow the directions on the box.

ASSEMBLE THE DISH:

- In a large baking or 'lasagna' dish, which you will have greased with lard or olive oil, spread a bit of the sugo over the bottom. Then cover the bottom with a layer of pasta. Since these pasta sheets are rather thick, avoid overlapping them. Trim the pasta with a knife or a pair of scissors, as needed. Then cover the pasta with a generous layer of sugo.

- Top the sugo with the polpettine, peas, and sausage pieces, and then with dabs of the ricotta cream here and there. Then place another layer of pasta and repeat, until you've used up your ingredients. Top with a generous dusting of grated parmesan cheese and a nice layer of sugo.

- Drizzle with olive oil.

SERVING THE LASAGNA:

- When done, remove the lasagna from the oven and allow to settle and cool for at least 30 minutes. In fact, I like to make lasagna ahead and reheat it gently, which gives it a rather firm texture and allows the flavors to meld beautifully.

CLASSIC MEAT LASAGNA

INGREDIENTS

- 1 pound sweet Italian sausage
- 1 pound lean ground beef
- 1 medium onion chopped
- 6 cloves garlic minced
- 28 ounces crushed tomatoes
- 12 ounces tomato paste
- 15 ounces tomato sauce
- ½ cup water
- ½ cup fresh chopped basil or 2 teaspoons dried basil
- 1 teaspoon Italian seasoning
- 1 teaspoon fennel seeds
- 1 ½ teaspoons salt
- ¼ teaspoon ground black pepper
- 4 Tablespoons chopped fresh parsley divided

INSTRUCTIONS

- 12 lasagna noodles regular
- 16 ounces ricotta cheese
- 1 egg
- ½ teaspoon salt
- Pinch of nutmeg
- ¾ pound freshly grated mozzarella cheese
- 1 cup freshly grated parmesan cheese

CREATING SAUCE

- Cook sausage, ground beef, onion, and garlic in a large dutch oven over medium heat until browned. Drain excess grease.

- Add crushed tomatoes, tomato paste, tomato sauce, and water. Add basil, fennel seeds, Italian seasoning, salt, pepper, and 2 tablespoons of the parsley. Reduce heat, cover, and simmer for 1 ½ hours, stirring occasionally.

INGREDIENTS

INSTRUCTIONS

- Preheat the oven to 375 degrees F. Don't bother cooking regular noodles. Just soak them in really hot tap water in the baking dish for 20-30 minutes before using rather than dirty another pot. They won't be fully cooked, but soft and will finish cooking in the oven. (Obviously you can cook them according to package directions if you prefer, though). No-cook noodles don't need to be cooked or soaked at all.

- Combine the ricotta cheese, egg, salt, nutmeg, and remaining parsley in a medium bowl. Spread 1 ½ cups of sauce in the bottom of a 9x13-inch baking dish. Lay lasagna noodles in a single layer over the sauce. Dollop half of the ricotta mixture over the noodles and spread in a thin, even layer. Sprinkle ⅓ of the mozzarella cheese and ¼ cup of the parmesan cheese. Spread with another 1 ½ cups of the sauce.

- Repeat with another layer of noodles, the remaining ricotta mixture, half of the remaining mozzarella cheese, and another ¼ cup of parmesan. Top with another 1 ½ cups of sauce.

- Top with a third, final layer of lasagna noodles, then cover with the remaining sauce. Sprinkle the remaining mozzarella and parmesan cheeses.

- Cover with foil then bake for 25 minutes. Remove foil and bake for another 25 minutes until the cheese is melted and starting to brown on top.

- Remove from the oven and let sit for at least 15 minutes before slicing and serving.

ARTICHOKE AND SPINACH CANNELLONI

Another dish that the recipe originated from my mother's family in Campania was Cannelloni. It was served around Easter and appeared on the "St. Joseph's Table" every March 19th. When my Momma made them, we ran to the table for dinner. It was definitely one of my favorite pasta dishes. We rarely ever ate it with meat stuffing, likely because of lack of money. This recipe brings together my fond memories and two of my absolute favorite vegetables –artichokes and spinach.

INGREDIENTS

- 3 Tablespoons olive oil
- 2 large artichoke hearts, peeled, quartered, and thinly sliced or ¾ lb whole cleaned hearts
- 1 onion, thinly sliced
- 2 garlic cloves, thinly sliced
- 1 teaspoon finely chopped rosemary
- ⅓ cup white wine
- ½ lb. spinach washed and drained
- 1 ⅔ cup heavy cream
- ¾ cup parmesan cheese, grated
- ½ teaspoon freshly grated nutmeg

INSTRUCTIONS

- **MAKE THE FILLING:**

Pour the olive oil into a large pan and cook the artichokes and onion over medium-high heat for 5 minutes, seasoning with salt and pepper. Stir occasionally to prevent it from burning. Add the garlic and rosemary and cook for another few minutes. Add the wine and ½ cup of water to soften the artichokes. Add the spinach, stirring until wilted. Add 1 1.4 cup of the heavy cream and bring to a boil. Boil for a few minutes and remove from the heat, then add the cheese and nutmeg. Check the seasoning for your taste.

- **MAKE THE PASTA:**

You can buy factory-made hard durum wheat shells or make the dough by thinly rolling out the dough into a 7 x 5 inch sheet. Be sure the grain of the pasta runs with the width not the length or the pasta will spit when rolled up.

- **COOK THE PASTA:**

Bring a saucepan of slate water to a boil and a dash of oil to prevent the sheets from sticking together. Blanch the pasta for 8 minutes and then drop into cold water. Spreads onto a dish towel in a single layer and blot excess water from both sides. Trim away torn edges, if needed.

- **TO ASSEMBLE:**

Preheat the oven to 350 degrees. Butter a 10-cup capacity dish. Lay out sheets of pasta on a work surface where you can spread out the filling and roll them into a tube. Put tubes into the dish, side-by-side, with the seam facing down. Pour the remaining cream and cheese on top.

Place the dish on a baking sheet in case the cream bubbles over. Bake for 30 minutes or until the top is golden brown. Remove from the oven and let it cook for 10 minutes before serving.

TRAPANESE PESTO

Trapanese pesto is a traditional Sicilian condiment, originated from Trapani. It is a raw sauce, usually pounded with a mortar.

It is said that it dates back to the time when Genoese ships that traded their products with the East docked in the port of Trapani. The northerners introduced Sicilians to pesto alla genovese, the classic basil pesto typical of Liguria. Having learned the Ligurian technique of grinding the fresh ingredients into a silky sauce, the Sicilians adapted the recipe with the use of fresh tomatoes and almonds native to the region. Busiate is a very popular pasta shape in Sicily, made with durum wheat semolina and water, the shape is made with a knitting needle. Bucatini is perfectly served with this pesto because the sauce gets trapped in the spirals of the long pasta so you enjoy the flavor with every bite.

PESTO ALLA TRAPANESE
(TRAPANI-STYLE TOMATO PESTO)

SERVES 6

INGREDIENTS

- 1 1/2 cups cherry tomatoes, very ripe & sweet
- 3 cups fresh basil leaves
- 1 garlic clove, peeled
- 1/2 cup almonds
- 1/3 cup Parmigiano Reggiano DOP or mild Pecorino, freshly grated
- 1/4 cup Extra Virgin Olive Oil
- Sea salt, to taste
- Garnish with pistachio (optional)

INSTRUCTIONS

- Add the tomatoes, extra virgin olive oil, almonds, and garlic to the bowl of a food processor, and mix for about two minutes.

- Add in the basil and pulse to combine. Do not mix too much, as this will help the basil retain its intensity of flavor and color.

- Remove from the mixer and fold in the grated cheese until creamy and thoroughly combined. Season with salt to taste.

- Serve and eat fresh, or keep in the fridge for up to two days. This pesto pairs especially well with pasta like busiate, penne, or spaghetti.

- Add chicken or shrimp to make it an entree. Here I simply sauteed shrimp and then added it to the pesto before I served it.

- Note: It is important not to cook the pesto, as the heat will alter the flavor and freshness of the ingredients. Add to freshly cooked pasta, but do not cook over heat.

- Storage: We can put it in the refrigerator for a few days. It should be covered with a little oil and tightly closed in special glass jars.

Bread and Pizza! Both are fundamental to Italian cuisine. Let's start by shattering a misconception: There is really no such thing as "Italian Bread." Like so many other foods, bread in Italy is specific to a particular region. There are well over 350 types of bread across Italy. Bread is a serious staple in Italy– it has been a part of Italy's cuisine since ancient times.

One regional difference in Italy's bread is the use of salt. In the Tuscany region, salt is not used when making bread. Long ago, the ruling class imposed a tax on salt. The citizens rebelled and the bakers decided they would not use salt in their bread. Therefore, they would not pay the tax. The tax was eventually lifted, but the bakers kept the no-salt bread. Growing up, our family mostly made simple peasant bread that we called Momma's bread. After living in Italy in 2014, I added a few Sicilian favorites, an olive bread from Puglia, focaccia from Genoa and simple flatbread.

PANE E PIZZA

Mangiamo | 65

MOM'S RUSTIC BREAD

INGREDIENTS

- 3 cups bread flour (or all-purpose flour)
- 1-1/2 cups cold water
- 1/4 teaspoon dry yeast
- A big pinch of salt, at least 1 Tbs

Tip: No worries if you don't have a standing mixer, you can just mix your dough in a normal bowl with a wooden spoon

INSTRUCTIONS

- Mix the dry ingredients in the bowl of a standing mixer, using the paddle. Then add the water in a drizzle until a very sticky dough has formed. If the dough seems dry, then add a bit more, a spoonful at a time. Take the bowl from the mixer and cover it with a towel and/or a plate and leave it in a warm (but not hot) place overnight. Scrape the dough out of the bowl with a spatula or wooden spoon onto a lightly floured surface. Flour your hands and form the mass of dough into a ball without kneading. Gingerly lay the dough on a lightly floured tea towel, then fold the ends of the towel on top of the dough. Let the bread rise again until it roughly doubles in size, which can take anywhere from 1 to 2 hours.

- About 30 minutes before the second rise is over, preheat your oven to 450F. Put a 4-1/2 or 5-1/2 quart cast iron casserole (about 10" in diameter) with its cover, in the oven to preheat along with the oven itself. Take the casserole out of the oven using your oven mitt and lay it on a heat-resistant surface. Remove the cover and lay it aside. Take the towel with the dough and quickly flip the dough into the casserole (it will go in 'upside down', which is fine). Shake the casserole, if need be, to center the dough and then quickly recover it.

- Put the casserole back in the oven and bake for 30 minutes. Then take it out of the oven and remove the cover. Put the casserole back into the oven, uncovered, and bake for another 15-20 minutes, until the bread has developed a beautiful golden brown crust. Turn the bread out onto a cooling rack and leave it until it has completely cooled. When the bread has cooled completely, after about 45 minutes to an hour, it is ready to enjoy!

OLIVE BREAD FROM PUGLIA

INGREDIENTS

- 3 cups all purpose flour
- 1/2 teaspoon instant yeast
- 1 1/2 cups kalamata and green olives, pitted
- 2 teaspoons dried thyme (or rosemary)
- 1 1/2 teaspoons salt
- 1/2 teaspoon black pepper
- 1 1/2 cups water

INSTRUCTIONS

- Combine all of the ingredients in a large mixing bowl. The dough will not be overly sticky but should come together. Add just a little water at a time if needed to incorporate all the flour. Cover the dough with plastic wrap and put a towel over the top to help it seal. Set the bowl aside for at least 8 hours to rise (I have gone as long as 24 hours).

- When ready to bake, heat the oven to 450F. Place a large cast iron pot (dutch oven) on the medium or medium-low rack while preheating for it to get hot. Use a spatula to scoop the dough into the hot pot. (If preferred, shape the dough on the counter during preheating, but I find it is easy to drop the dough in a rough circle straight into the pot).

- Place the lid on the pot and cook at 450 F for 30 minutes.

- Remove the lid and let cook for an additional 15 minutes to further brown. If it looks or smells done sooner, remove from the oven sooner. Let the bread cool completely on a cooling rack.

- **NOTES**

This makes one large loaf of rustic bread, which is much more dense than a French bread. If your bread is cooking too fast on the bottom which commonly happens to me, place a baking sheet on a rack lower than the pot to help disperse heat that is coming from the bottom.

CIABATTA
(NO-KNEAD CIABATTA RECIPE)

INGREDIENTS

- 3 ½ cups white bread flour
- ½ cup whole wheat bread flour
- 1 ½ teaspoons salt
- ¼ teaspoon active dry yeast
- 2 cups water
- 1 tablespoon olive oil
- 2 tablespoons cornmeal

INSTRUCTIONS

- Place white and wheat flour in a large bowl. Add salt, yeast, and water. Mix until a wet sticky dough comes together, about 5 minutes. Scrape down the sides of the bowl. Cover with foil. Allow dough to rise for 18 hours at room temperature. It should not be too warm. Punch dough down with a spatula and fold it over a few times.

- Lightly grease a heavy-rimmed baking sheet with olive oil. Sprinkle generously with cornmeal. Lightly spray a work surface with water. Place a long sheet of plastic wrap on the damp surface to hold it in place. Sprinkle plastic wrap with flour. Scrape the dough onto the floured surface. Sprinkle flour on top of the dough. Gently stretch and pull dough into a long, flat rectangular shape, 12 to 15 inches long. Bring a plastic sheet to the edge of the prepared pan and flip the dough into the prepared pan. Reshape the dough, if necessary. Dust with flour.

- Cover with a light dry towel. Let rise for about 2 hours. Preheat the oven to 425 degrees F (220 degrees C). Bake dough in a preheated oven until the loaf is nicely browned, 35 to 45 minutes.

ROSEMARY FOCACCIA

INGREDIENTS

- Makes 2 loaves (8- or 9-inch pie plates or a 9×13-inch pan)
- 4 cups all-purpose flour or bread flour
- 2 teaspoons kosher salt
- 2 teaspoons instant yeast, see notes above if using active dry
- 2 cups lukewarm water, made by combining 1/2 cup boiling water with 1 1/2 cups cold water
- butter or lard for greasing
- 4 tablespoons olive oil, divided
- flaky sea salt, such as Maldon
- 1 to 2 teaspoons whole rosemary leaves, optional

INSTRUCTIONS

- Make the dough: In a large bowl, whisk together the flour, salt, and instant yeast. Add the water. Using a rubber spatula, mix until the liquid is absorbed and the ingredients form a sticky dough ball. Rub the surface of the dough lightly with olive oil. Cover the bowl with a damp tea towel, cloth bowl cover, or plastic wrap and place in the refrigerator immediately for at least 12 hours or for as long as three days.

- Line the pans or pan with parchment paper or grease with butter or lard. Pour a tablespoon of oil into the center of each pan or 2 tablespoons of oil if using the 9×13-inch pan. Using two forks, deflate the dough by releasing it from the sides of the bowl and pulling it toward the center. Rotate the bowl in quarter turns as you deflate, turning the mass into a rough ball. Use the forks to split the dough into two equal pieces (or do not split if using the 9×13-inch pan). Place one piece into one of the prepared pans. Roll the dough ball in the oil to coat it all over, forming a rough ball. Repeat with the remaining piece. Let the dough balls rest for 3 to 4 hours depending on the temperature of your kitchen.

INSTRUCTIONS

- Set a rack in the middle of the oven and preheat it to 425°F. If using the rosemary, sprinkle it over the dough. Pour a tablespoon of oil over each round of dough (or two tablespoons if using a 9×13-inch pan). Rub your hands lightly in the oil to coat, then, using all of your fingers, press straight down to create deep dimples. If necessary, gently stretch the dough as you dimple to allow the dough to fill the pan. Sprinkle it with flaky sea salt all over.

- Transfer the pans or pan to the oven and bake for 25 to 30 minutes, until the underside is golden and crisp. Remove the pans or pan from the oven and transfer the focaccia to a cooling rack. Let it cool for 10 minutes before cutting and serving; let it cool completely if you are halving it with the intention of making a sandwich.

ITALIAN FLATBREAD

INGREDIENTS

- 1.5 cups 00 flour or all-purpose flour
- ½ cup warm water
- ½ tbsp olive oil
- 1 tsp baking powder
- ¼ tsp salt

This flatbread is a soft and fluffy bread that can be filled with anything you like from cured meats, cheese and grilled veggies. So delicious, easy to make and yeast free, perfect for lunch or a snack!

INSTRUCTIONS

- Add the flour, baking powder and salt to a bowl, stir so everything is evenly mixed through. Make a well in the flour and add the water and olive oil. Stir everything together to form a dough. Tip the dough onto a lightly floured surface and knead to form a smooth ball (make sure not to over knead the dough.) Wrap the dough in plastic wrap (cling film) and let it rest at room temperature for 30 minutes.

- Pre-heat a large round skillet or frying pan on the stove. Divide the dough in four and roll each piece into a thin round flatbread shape (don't worry if they aren't perfectly round). Heat each flatbread one at a time on the skillet, once it's puffed up and looks golden, turn it over and cook on the other side. It should take around 2 minutes each side. Fill each flatbread with your desired fillings and fold in half.

- **Tip:** To keep them soft - place the flatbreads on a plate and wrap them with a clean kitchen towel to help keep them soft.

BRIOCHE

INGREDIENTS

- Makes 12 (3 ozs. each)
- Ingredients
- 3/4 cup milk plus 1 tbsp for the egg wash
- 8 grams active dry yeast (1 packet)
- 4 large eggs (reserve 1 for the egg wash)
- 1/2 cup sugar
- 3 tsp honey
- 1 tsp vanilla extract
- 1 orange, zested
- 1/3 cup butter cubed and at room temperature
- 4 cups all-purpose flour
- 1 tsp salt

INSTRUCTIONS

- Warm the milk until lukewarm. Place yeast and 1 tsp sugar (taken from the total amount of sugar) in a bowl. Pour the warm milk over the yeast and sugar and let sit for 10 minutes until foamy.

- Meanwhile, in the bowl of your mixer fitted with the paddle attachment, mix 3 eggs and sugar together until smooth, about 1 minute. Add the honey; vanilla extract, and orange zest. Mix on the low setting until just combined. Pour in the yeast mixture and mix. Add the softened butter cut into cubes and mix to combine. The butter will not dissolve into the yeast mixture at this point, this is normal.

- Remove the paddle attachment and replace with a dough hook. With the mixer running at the lowest setting, begin adding flour 1/2 cup at a time as well as the salt. Scrape the sides of the bowl with a spatula to incorporate all of the flour. When all of the flour has been added, increase the speed to the next setting and knead the dough for 10 minutes.

- The dough will be sticky and wrap itself around the dough hook. Do not add more flour to it. Use a spatula to scrape the dough into a lightly greased bowl. Cover with plastic wrap and place in a warm part of the kitchen to rise for 3 hours, until doubled in bulk.

INSTRUCTIONS

- Shape the brioche

- Line 2 baking sheets with parchment paper.

- Use a kitchen scale to divide the dough into 12 (3 oz.) balls.

- Let rise for 2 hours until doubled in bulk. Preheat to 350 degrees F.

- Bake for 15 minutes, until the brioche is golden brown. Serve warm or at room temperature.

SICILIAN GRISSINI

INGREDIENTS

- 2 cups bread flour spooned and leveled
- 1 tsp sugar
- 1.5 tsp fine sea salt
- 1 tsp fast-action yeast
- 2 tbsp olive oil
- ¾ cup warm water
- semolina, for dusting

Long, thin, and crispy homemade Italian breadsticks are perfectly served with drinks, cured meats, and cheese for an aperitivo or for dunking in dips or soup, so delicious and easy to make at home!

INSTRUCTIONS

- Place the flour, sugar and salt in a mixing bowl and stir together. Make a well in the middle and add the yeast, warm water and olive oil. Stir everything together until a rough dough forms then tip out onto a clean work surface. Knead the dough until it's smooth and elastic. You'll probably need to sprinkle the work surface lightly with flour as you knead the dough if it's sticking. Shape the dough into a ball and place in a clean bowl dusted lightly with flour. Cover with plastic wrap and let the dough rest for 15 minutes.

- After the dough has rested, remove it from the bowl and press it gently to form a rectangle. Fold one edge lengthwise into the middle of the dough then fold the opposite edge right over so it overlaps the first fold right to the opposite end, it should resemble a log. Turn the log over and gently push each end in so it resembles a rough rectangle. Place the dough on a baking tray brushed with olive oil. Brush the top of the dough with more olive oil and loosely top with plastic wrap.

INSTRUCTIONS

- Leave the dough to prove for 1 hour or until doubled in size. Pre-heat the oven to 450F . Lightly sprinkle semolina over the baking tray and sprinkle a little more over the uncovered dough.

- Using a pizza cutter or sharp knife cut ¼ inch (1cm) thick strip widthwise from the dough. Gently stretch the dough into a long breadstick long enough to fit your tray. Continue with the rest of the dough until your tray is filled with breadsticks making sure to keep a small gap between each one so they aren't touching.

- Bake in the oven for 12-15 minutes or until lightly golden. Let cool completely before serving.

- Texture - the full cooking time will give you crunchy and crisp breadsticks if you'd like them a little softer, then cook them for around 5 minutes less.

- Storage - They will keep well in an airtight container for 5-7 days. If they start to turn slightly soft or chewy you can pop them back in a hot oven for 5 minutes to crisp up

- Freezing - these breadsticks can be frozen in plastic freezer bags, containers or tightly wrapped in plastic wrap and aluminum foil. Thaw completely before serving, you can pop them in a hot oven to heat up if desired.

Mangiamo | 75

SICILIAN PIZZA SFINCIONE

Growing up, we ate only Sicilian-style pizza called Sfincione. I know what you are thinking: your family comes from Naples, the most famous pizza ever! But we used a traditional Sicilian recipe, which is more like bread than a tossed pizza. Our nonna's recipe was GOLD to all of us, and it was a right of passage to get in the kitchen with Nonna to learn how to make it.

You would never leave home, venturing into adulthood without that recipe; and the recipe for S cookies and fig cookies. Christmas Eve and Sunday dinner were not complete without Sfincione. To this day, I love it much more than American-style pizza. In fact, I don't enjoy a pizza with gobs of melted mozzarella and loads of toppings. I am proud to share this special recipe with you. Benvenuto in famiglia!

(Welcome to the family!)

SICILIAN PIZZA SFINCIONE

SERVINGS: 16 THICK SLICES

2 BAKING TRAYS 13X9 INCH

Sicilian Pizza, aka Sfincione, is made with a thick, soft rectangular pizza crust, a rich tomato sauce flavored with onions and anchovies, and topped with breadcrumbs.

INGREDIENTS

THE DOUGH

- 4 cups 00 flour
- 1 ⅓ cup lukewarm water
- 2 tsp fast-action yeast
- 2 tbsp olive oil plus extra for greasing
- ½ tsp sugar
- ½ tsp salt

THE SAUCE

- 1 tbsp olive oil
- 1 white onion thinly sliced
- 7-8 salted anchovies
- 28 oz canned plum tomatoes can also use pureed tomatoes or canned chopped tomatoes
- ½ cup caciocavallo cheese cubed, can also use provolone, pecorino or mild gouda
- Salt and pepper to taste

BREADCRUMB TOPPING

- ¼ cup breadcrumbs
- ¼ cup freshly grated pecorino or parmesan
- 1 tsp dried oregano
- 1 tsp olive oil

INSTRUCTIONS

- Add the flour to a large mixing bowl and add the sugar, salt and yeast making sure to not place the yeast directly on the salt.

- Stir to combine the dried ingredients then make a well in the center and add the warm water and olive oil.

- Stir to form a dough then tip out onto a clean work surface lightly dusted with flour. Knead the dough for 10 minutes until smooth and elastic then place in a clean bowl lightly greased with a little olive oil. Cover with plastic wrap and leave to proof for around 3 hours or until tripled in size.

- Meanwhile, make the sauce, add the olive oil to a large pan or skillet on a medium heat. Add the sliced onion and saute slowly until soft and translucent (5-10 minutes). Once soft add the anchovies and stir, breaking them up as they cook. Saute the onions and anchovies for 5 minutes. Add the tomatoes and simmer the sauce for 15 minutes.

INSTRUCTIONS

- Next, add the cubed cheese with a pinch of salt and pepper and continue to cook the sauce for another 10 minutes, set aside to cool.

- After the dough has risen, tip it out into a clean work surface lightly dusted with flour and divide into two. Roll each half of the dough out into a rectangle big enough to fit a 13x9 inch baking tray, it should be around ½ inch thick.

- Lightly grease the baking tray with olive oil and place the dough in the tray. Top with half of the prepared sauce making sure to spread it out to the edges. Repeat with the second pizza.

- Cover with plastic wrap and leave to proof for a second time for two hours or until doubled in size. Preheat the oven to 450F.

- Mix the breadcrumbs, grated pecorino, dried oregano, and olive oil in a bowl, then sprinkle over each pizza. Bake in the oven for 25-30 minutes, let rest for 5 minutes, then cut into slices and serve.

- Make sure to let the dough prove for long enough, it needs to triple in size with the first proof then rise again in the baking tray for at least 1-2 hours. This will ensure your crust is thick and light.

- When you move the dough to the baking tray to prove, add the toppings at the same time so you don't knock any air out later.

- Bake this pizza at the highest temperature your oven will go for best results! After baking, let the pizza rest for 5 minutes before cutting.

BEST BASIC PIZZA DOUGH RECIPE
2 LARGE PIZZAS

The best basic pizza dough that's my go-to recipe for anytime I want to make pizzas or even focaccia. It's so simple and takes around 10 minutes to make, it's the best way to make homemade pizzas!

INGREDIENTS

- 4 cups 00 flour
- 2 tsp 7g fast action dried yeast
- 1 1/3 cups lukewarm water
- 1 1/2 tbsp olive oil
- 1 pinch pinch salt
- 1/2 tsp sugar

INSTRUCTIONS

- Add the yeast to the lukewarm water with ½ teaspoon sugar and set aside for 5 minutes. Combine the flour and salt in a large mixing bowl. Make a well in the center and add the yeast and water and start to mix it together with a metal spoon. Add the olive oil and mix together until a rough dough forms. If it's too sticky you can gradually add a little more flour.

- Dust a clean work surface with a little flour and knead the dough for around 5-10 minutes until it's silky smooth and soft. If you lightly press your finger on the ball of dough it should spring back up easily. Add ½ tablespoon of olive oil to a large clean bowl and rub all over until the bowl is coated. Shape the dough into a ball and place in the bowl, rub the top of the dough with a tiny amount of olive oil. Cover with cling film and leave in a warm place for at least 2-3 hours or until doubled in size.

TIP: You can add any toppings you desire. Roll out thin or pan style, which is thicker. Here are a few ideas or favorites we make. (See Page 80)

Vegetable Pizza with thin crust

Smoked ham with figs with Pan - Style Crust

Cherry Tomatoes with Argula with Pan -Style Crust

My father's family comes from Prizzi in the province of Palermo, Sicily. Prizzi is a small village located on the top of the Sicani Mountains. Our daily cuisine was similar to life in Sicily with plenty of grains, vegetables, and fish. Meat was used in very special dishes and Sunday meals, not served everyday.

Our Sicilian vegetable dishes are the star with meat used to create complex flavors. Among the most used vegetables are eggplant, zucchini, peppers, cauliflower, broccoli and artichoke. We raised our own chickens and rabbits in the backyard so that was a major source of protein. We used the cheaper cuts of pork and beef, which were ground or stewed in a sauce to soften the meat. Here are a few of my family favorites.

RICETTE DI FAMIGLIA SICILIANE

Palermo, Italy

Mangiamo | 81

Home-made Sicilian Pork Sausage with Fennel

Salsiccia al vino

HOME-MADE SICILIAN PORK SAUSAGE WITH FENNEL

SERVES 8

INGREDIENTS

- 1.75 lbs. pork shoulder
- ½ lb pork fat
- 1 tbsp salt
- 2 tbsp fennel seeds
- ½ cup red or white wine
- 1 tbsp freshly ground pepper
- Edible sausage casing

INSTRUCTIONS

- Roughly chop the pork and fat and then grind. Put the ground meat in a bowl. Add the salt, wine, fennel seeds, and ground pepper and knead well. Stuff the sausage into the casing and tie it off with a bubble knot. Let it dry in the fridge overnight before cooking (or freezing) it.

- This sausage can be frozen for up to 3 months, just wrap it in foil and then put it into a Ziploc bag before freezing it.

SALSICCIA AL VINO

SERVES 6

INGREDIENTS

- 2 lbs. pork sausage (see home-made Sicilian Pork Sausage with Fennel recipe)
- ½ cup grapes
- ¼ cup pine nuts
- 1 white onion, chopped
- I bottle of a good red wine
- 2 sprigs of rosemary
- 2 or 3 sage leaves
- 1 tbsp honey
- 1 red pepper, sliced
- Extra virgin olive oil
- Salt to taste

INSTRUCTIONS

- Chop the sage leaves and rosemary sprigs with the scissors. Rinse grapes and cut them in half. In a large saucepan, brown the onion in a tablespoon of oil for 2 minutes and add herbs. Add the sausage and brown all sides. Pour the red wine until it is half covered, put a lid on and cook over low heat.

- When half of the cooking liquid is reduced, turn the sausage over, then add the sliced red pepper, grapes, pine nuts and honey. Cook for 10 more minutes.

- Serve as an appetizer or with potatoes as a meal.

Mangiamo | 83

SICILY'S SECRET SAUCE: AGRODOLCE

(AH-GROH-DOLE-CHAY) SWEET-AND-SOUR

SERVES 8

INGREDIENTS

- 2 tablespoons extra virgin olive oil
- 1 small shallot, minced
- 2 garlic cloves, minced
- ½ cup red wine vinegar
- 1 tablespoon capers
- ¼ cup pine nuts
- ¼ cup dried fruit (preferably golden raisins, dried cranberries, and dried apricots)
- 3 tablespoons honey
- ½ teaspoon salt (Kosher salt or sea salt)
- Pinch of black pepper
- 3 tablespoons unsalted butter, at room temperature
- Lemon zest (optional)
- Red pepper flakes (optional)
- Fresh chiles (optional)
- Fresh parsley (optional)

YOU CAN USE AGRODOLCE AS THE FOLLOWING:

- **AS A CONDIMENT:**

Serve agrodolce on brussels sprouts, asparagus, broccoli, and other vegetables, especially roasted vegetables. Or use the agrodolce as a condiment on a charcuterie board.

- **AS A SANDWICH SPREAD:**

Add the sauce to slices of bread before you layer your meats and cheeses. The acidity in the agrodolce cuts through the fatty meats, creating a nice balance of flavor.

- **FINISH DRESSING MEATS:**

The agrodolce adds sweetness and a sticky texture that complements the smoky char on grilled meats or other grilled side dishes.

INSTRUCTIONS

- Heat a small saucepan over medium heat and add the olive oil. Add the garlic and shallots and sauté until they become slightly golden brown, about 5 minutes. Add the red wine vinegar and simmer that mixture until it reduces by half, about 5 minutes.

- Next, add the capers, dried fruits, and pine nuts. Stir to combine everything. Stir the honey into the rest of the mixture and simmer everything for about 4 minutes, until the sauce is thicker.

- Add the butter and stir until it's fully combined with the rest of the sauce. Then add the salt and pepper, stirring again to combine all the ingredients. Add any other optional flavorings, such as lemon zest, red pepper flakes, fresh chiles, or fresh parsley.

- Agrodolce is this sweet but sour sauce. It is good to keep on hand and use as a condiment, a sandwich spread, or to finish grilled meats. Agrodolce means sweet and sour and is one of the signature flavors of the Sicilian kitchen. Made by simmering capers, pine nuts, raisins, fresh mint, wine vinegar, and sugar with meat, fish, or vegetables, variations on agrodolce are made all over the island.

"This dish is one of my favorite meals. Rabbit pieces are cooked with this sweet and sour sauce until it is tender. tender. If you prefer, you can use chicken. But I promise you, the rabbit makes it special."

Chef Margie Raimondo

CONIGLIO IN AGRODOLCE

INGREDIENTS

- 3 thyme sprigs, plus extra to serve
- ¼ cup white wine vinegar
- 2 ⅛ cup water
- ¼ cup raisins
- 1 tablespoon sour cherries
- ½ cup of eggplant
- 1 cup of peppers, red or yellow
- ¼ cup pine nuts, toasted
- ¼ cup) walnuts, toasted chopped
- 2/4 cup dark chocolate, (70% cocoa solids) finely chopped
- 1 rabbit cut into 8 pieces
- ½ cup plain flour
- ¼ cup olive oil
- 1 carrot, finely chopped
- 1 celery stalk, finely chopped
- 1 small brown onion, finely chopped
- 6 garlic cloves, finely chopped
- ¼ cup butter
- ⅓ lb. prosciutto, chopped
- 2 juniper berries
- 5 black peppercorns

INSTRUCTIONS

- Season the rabbit with salt and pepper, toss in the flour to coat, and shake off excess. Heat oil in a large deep frying pan over high heat. Cook rabbit, turning, for 5 minutes or until golden. Transfer to a plate using a slotted spoon. Reduce heat to medium, add carrot, celery, onion, garlic, and butter, and cook, stirring, for 5 minutes or until the onion is lightly golden.

- Add prosciutto, juniper berries, peppercorns, peppers, eggplant and thyme, and cook for a further minute or until fragrant. Return rabbit to pan and add sugar, vinegar, and water. Bring to a boil, then reduce heat to low and cook. covered for 45 minutes or until the rabbit is tender.

- Add raisins, cherries, nuts and chocolate. and cook, stirring occasionally, for 5 minutes or until chocolate is melted and sauce is slightly reduced. Season and top with extra thyme sprigs to serve.

Baked Fish with Creamy Lemon Sauce

Serves 4

INGREDIENTS

- 1/4 cup unsalted butter melted.
- 2-3 tablespoons capers
- 2 Tablespoons lemon juice
- 2-3 large garlic cloves.= 1 teaspoon
- 1/2 teaspoon Italian seasoning
- 1/4 teaspoon salt
- 1/4 teaspoon cumin
- 1/4 teaspoon black pepper
- 1/2 cup heavy cream
- 1 pound cod fish filets

INSTRUCTIONS

- Preheat the oven to 400F.
- In your baking dish, add all the ingredients except for fish and mix well.
- Add in fish filets and toss to coat.
- Sprinkle top with more salt and pepper.
- Bake for 12-15 minutes until flaky or cod registers between 130 and 140F.
- Garnish with fresh parsley and lemon slices.

NOTES

- Use any white fish filets you like .
- This recipe works great with snapper.
- If using frozen fish, let them thaw completely and pat dry with a paper kitchen towel.

CHICKEN SPIEDINI - ITALIAN CHICKEN SKEWERS

SERVES 4

Special Equipment
- 4 wooden or metal skewers
- (If using wooden skewers, soak them in a tray of water for 30 minutes)

INGREDIENTS

- 4 chicken breasts
- 2 tbsp fresh rosemary finely chopped
- 1 tbsp dried oregano
- Zest of 1 whole lemon
- 2 tbsp olive oil
- Salt and pepper to season
- Squeeze of fresh lemon juice for serving

INSTRUCTIONS

- Cut the chicken into 1-inch cubed pieces and add to a bowl.

- Add all the herbs, zest, olive oil, and a good pinch of salt and pepper. Stir until thoroughly combined. You can use the chicken immediately or place it in the fridge to marinate until you're ready.

- Heat the broiler (grill) to high. Thread the chicken onto the wooden skewers evenly and place it on a baking tray. Place the chicken on a high shelf under the broiler and cook for 5 minutes; turn the skewers and cook for another 5 minutes until browned and cooked through.

- Serve the chicken skewers on a plate with a squeeze of lemon juice and some grilled veggies.

- Cut the chicken into even pieces, so they all cook at the same time. Feel free to play around with flavors using different herbs and spices; these are so versatile! You can grill these outdoors during the summer, giving them an extra smoky flavor.

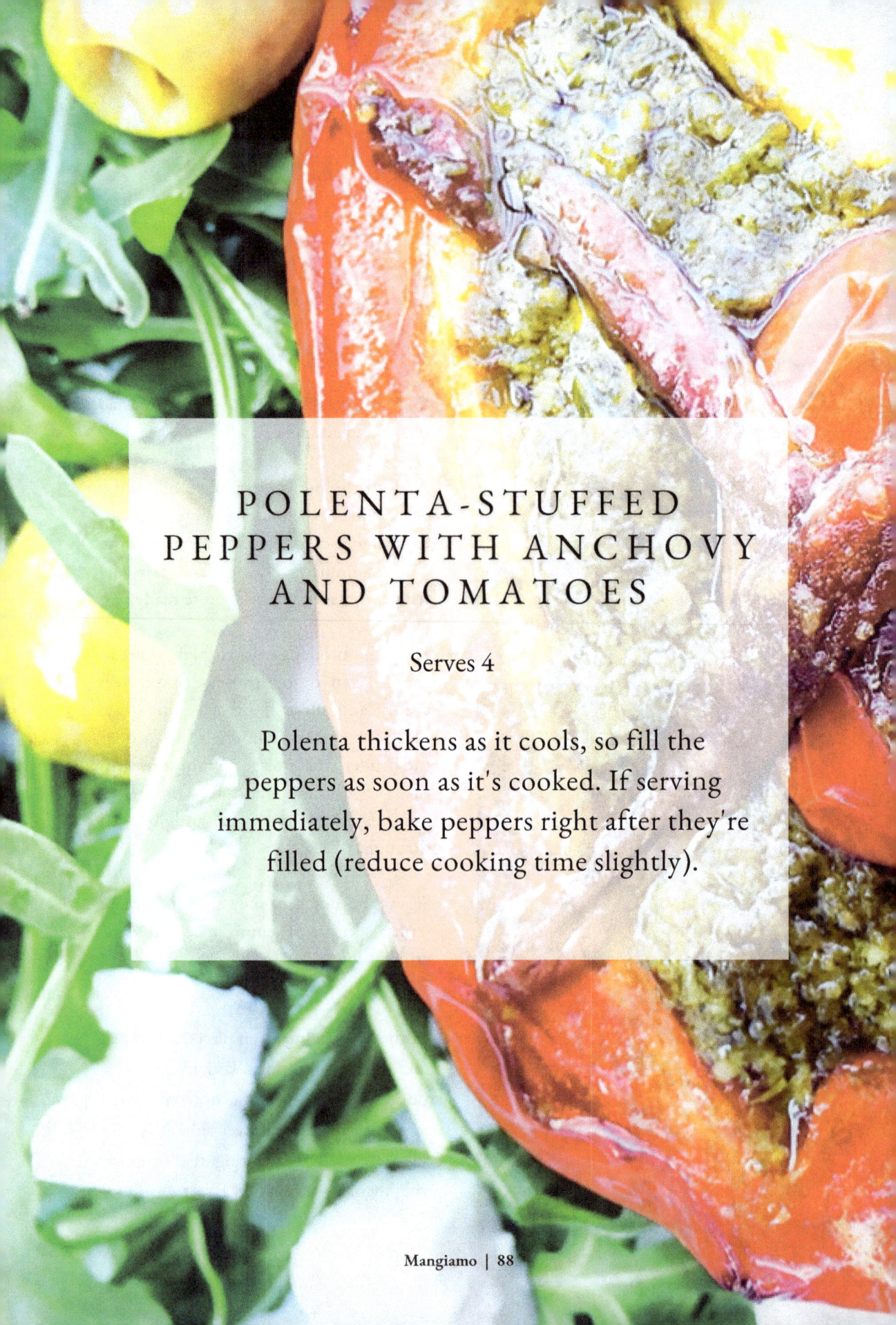

POLENTA-STUFFED PEPPERS WITH ANCHOVY AND TOMATOES

Serves 4

Polenta thickens as it cools, so fill the peppers as soon as it's cooked. If serving immediately, bake peppers right after they're filled (reduce cooking time slightly).

INGREDIENTS

- 4 tablespoons butter
- 1 onion, finely chopped
- 1 1/2 teaspoons finely chopped fresh rosemary (or 3/4 teaspoon dried rosemary, crumbled)
- Coarse salt and ground pepper
- 1/2 cup yellow cornmeal
- 1 package (10 ounces) of frozen corn kernels, thawed
- 1 cup shredded sharp white cheddar cheese
- 4 red bell peppers, halved lengthwise through stem, ribs and seeds removed
- 1/c cup of pesto
- 2 anchovies per pepper
- 1 cherry tomato per pepper

INSTRUCTIONS

- In a medium saucepan, melt 1 tablespoon butter over medium-high. Cook onion, stirring often, until lightly browned, 5 minutes. Add 3 cups water, rosemary, 2 teaspoons salt, and 1/4 teaspoon pepper; bring to a boil.

- Whisking constantly, gradually add cornmeal, whisking until incorporated before adding more. Reduce to a simmer; cook, whisking frequently, until thickened, about 5 minutes. Remove from heat; stir in corn, remaining 3 tablespoons butter, and half the cheese until melted.

- Place peppers in a large baking dish; fill with polenta mixture. Cool to room temperature. Cover tightly with foil; refrigerate until ready to use, up to 2 days.

- Preheat the oven to 400 degrees. Pour 1/2 cup water on the bottom of the baking dish. Cover with foil; bake for 30 minutes. Remove foil; sprinkle with remaining cheese. Add a tablespoon of pesto, 2 anchovies, criss-crossed, and a cherry tomato.

- Return to the oven; bake, uncovered, until the cheese is golden and the peppers are very tender, about 30 minutes more. Serve immediately.

angiamo | 89

POLPETTONE
Italian Meatloaf wrapped in Pancetta

INGREDIENTS

- 4.5 cups 12% fat ground beef
- 1.5 cups 5% fat ground pork
- ½ cup milk
- 3 large slices crustless bread or the inside of a crusty bread
- ½ cup white wine
- 2 large cloves garlic crushed
- ½ tablespoon dried oregano
- 1 tablespoon fresh rosemary finely chopped
- 1 large egg
- ½ cup grated parmesan
- 1 pinch nutmeg
- 1 tsp fine salt
- 1 pinch ground pepper

THE FILLING

- 7 oz pancetta strips or bacon - around 20 strips
- 7 oz Taleggio, rinds removed
- ½ ball fresh mozzarella (2.1oz/60g)

INGREDIENTS FOR THE SAUCE

- 28 oz canned chopped tomatoes high quality
- 1 small handful fresh basil
- 1 clove garlic
- 1 tablespoon olive oil
- Salt and pepper

- You can make the sauce while the meatloaf is cooking then heat it up before serving (it only takes 10-15 minutes to make)

- Add the olive oil to a large pan and add the finely chopped garlic. Saute for around a minute until fragrant.

- Next, add the canned tomatoes. Add around 1 tablespoon of water to the cans, rinse out any leftover tomato and add it to the sauce. Crush the tomatoes with a potato masher for a smoother sauce.

- Simmer for 10-15 minutes until reduced slightly. Add torn fresh basil, stir and set aside.

Instructions for Meatloaf

- Lay a large sheet of plastic wrap on a clean work surface and lay two rows of pancetta lengthways on top. Make sure the second row of pancetta overlaps the first by 2 inches (see step by step photos for reference). Put the meatloaf mixture on top of the pancetta and flatten it into a rough rectangle shape.

- Cut the taleggio and mozzarella into cubes or strips and add it along the middle of the meat. Shape the meat over the cheese into a large log. Spend a minute or two smoothing out and sealing all the cracks around the meatloaf. This is an important step to stop the cheese from oozing out. Next, wrap the pancetta all around the meatloaf tucking in the ends tightly. Keep it wrapped in plastic wrap and refrigerate for at least 30 minutes.

- Once ready, preheat the oven to 350F. Remove the meatloaf and place on a large baking tray and tie it firmly with kitchen string (one large loop around the length and 7-8 loops around the width). This gives the meatloaf extra support to keep the cheese in the middle. Bake in the oven for 80 minutes until cooked through and crispy on the outside.

- The meatloaf will keep well (covered) in the fridge for up to 4-5 days. Enjoy it cold or reheat it in the oven.

SCALOPPINE AL MARSALA
(Veal in Marsala Wine)

SERVES 4

- 1 lb thin slices of veal, beef or chicken
- 1//4 cup of butter
- Flour
- Dry Marsala wine
- Salt and pepper

- Tenderize the slices of meat and brush with the flour. Melt the butter in a frying pan and cook slowly, adding a little salt and pepper. When cooked, remove the meat and leave in a hot place.

- Add a glass of Marsala to the frying pan and stir until the sauce is a liquid cream. Pour the sauce on the veal and serve with new potatoes and a seasonal vegetable.

MY MAMA'S FRIED BACCALÀ

I love everything about Baccalà!

We ate it fried on Christmas Eve and other Sunday family dinners. It was usually available in the ethnic grocery stores around Los Angeles. I learned new recipes during my travels in Spain and Portugal. Here are my absolute favorite recipes.

- **READY TO FRY:**

Adjust oven rack to middle position and preheat oven to 200°F). Set a wire rack inside a rimmed baking sheet and line with paper towels. In a large Dutch oven, heat oil over medium-high heat to 375°F. (see procedure on page 93)

LEARNING TECHNIQUES
How to prepare
SALTED COD FOR COOKING

- Cut the salted cod into pieces that are 6 inches long, and 1 1/2 to 2 inches wide.
- Soak the pieces of salted cod in a bowl of material resistant to salt, best if glass or ceramic.
- Cover the bowl with plastic wrap and store into the fridge.
- Replace the water into the bowl every 12 hours
- After 48 hours, cut a little piece of salted cod and boil it for a minute, then taste to check if it is still too salty.
- If the salted cod is still too salty, extend the soak 24 hours more, replacing the water every 8-10 hours.
- Cook the cod immediately after soaking.

INSTRUCTIONS

- Meanwhile, in a large bowl, whisk together flour, cornstarch, and baking powder until well-combined. Add sparkling water and vodka and, using chopsticks, stir until a batter just forms. Don't over-mix; a few lumps of flour are fine. Add half of the salt cod to batter. If you have a mixture of thick filets and thin tail pieces, keep them separate and batter the thick filets first. Submerge pieces to evenly coat them in batter. Working with one piece at a time, lift cod from batter, allowing any excess batter to drip back into the bowl, and carefully add to hot oil, lowering it gently from as close to the oil's surface as possible to minimize splashing; repeat with remaining battered pieces of cod.

- Fry cod, turning occasionally, until batter is golden brown and crisp on all sides, 5 to 6 minutes for thin tail pieces, 7 to 8 minutes for thick filets. Using a spider skimmer or slotted spoon, transfer cod to the prepared wire rack, season very lightly with salt, and transfer to the oven to keep warm.

MEDITERRANEAN-STYLE BACCALÀ

MEDITERRANEAN-STYLE BACCALÀ

SERVES 4

INGREDIENTS

- 2 pounds Baccalà
- Salt and freshly ground pepper
- Juice of 1 large lemon
- 2 tablespoons extra virgin olive oil
- 1 pound onions, cut in half lengthwise and then sliced thinly across the grain
- 2 large garlic cloves, minced or puréed
- 1 28-ounce can be chopped tomatoes with juice (in summer use 2 pounds grated or peeled seeded ripe tomatoes)
- ⅛ teaspoon sugar
- 1 teaspoon sweet paprika
- ⅛ teaspoon cinnamon
- 1 tablespoon tomato paste dissolved in 1/4 cup water
- ½ cup dry white wine or red wine
- Leaves from 1 bunch flat-leaf parsley, chopped (about 1/2 cup)

OTHER OPTIONAL ACCOMPANIMENTS

- You can make the tomato sauce up to 3 days ahead. Bring back to a simmer before proceeding with the fish.

INSTRUCTIONS

- Pat the fish dry and season to taste with salt and pepper. Oil one or two baking dishes large enough to accommodate the fish in one layer. Lay the fish in the dish and pour on the lemon juice. Refrigerate for 30 to 60 minutes while you prepare the remaining ingredients.

- Preheat the oven to 375 degrees. Heat the oil over medium heat in a large, heavy skillet and add the onions. Cook, stirring often, until they have softened and begun to color slightly, 8 to 10 minutes. Add a generous pinch of salt and the garlic and cook, stirring, until the garlic is fragrant, 30 seconds to a minute. Stir in the tomatoes, sugar, paprika, cinnamon, dissolved tomato paste, wine, half the parsley and more salt and pepper to taste and bring to a simmer.

- Simmer uncovered, stirring often, until the sauce has cooked down a bit and is very fragrant, about 15 minutes. Remove from the heat and pour over the fish. Sprinkle on the remaining parsley.

- Place in the oven and bake until the fish is opaque and pulls apart easily with a fork, about 30 minutes. Baste the fish every 10 minutes if it is not submerged in the sauce. Serve hot or warm, with rice, bulgur, or potatoes.

BACCALÀ MANTECATO

This is my recipe adapted from a classic Italian whipped salt cod recipe from Venice. I add the chickpeas to give it more texture and flavor.

INGREDIENTS

- 1.5 pounds salted Baccalà
- 2 garlic cloves, minced
- 1/2 cup heavy cream
- 1/2 cup olive oil
- 3/4 cups of cooked chickpeas
- Salt and pepper to taste

preparing cooked chickpeas see page 24

chickpeas

INSTRUCTIONS

- Use the Baccalà once it has soaked for at least 48 hours. Now place in a pot and cook for 30 minutes. Drain the water, and remove the skin and any large bones. Break the fish into pieces and place in a mixer/food processor.

- Add half of the chickpeas, olive oil, garlic cloves, and cream to the mixer/food processor and mix until it reaches a smooth and even consistency. Now stir in the remaining chickpeas.

- Season to taste with salt and pepper and serve on slices of baguette. Garnish with mint or basil.

SHOPPING List

COOKING INSTRUCTIONS
SPANISH COD FRITTERS

MAKE THE BATTER

- Pour water and oil in a saucepan and bring to a boil over medium heat. Shake in the flour slowly and stir with a wooden spoon to make a batter.

- Remove the pan from the heat and continue beating the batter for 2 to 3 minutes to cool it. Add the eggs one at a time, incorporating completely after each addition. Add the cod mixture to the pan and stir to combine. Let the batter cool to room temperature.

FRY THE FRITTERS

Heat 3 inches of the oil in a high-sided saucepan over medium-high heat until it reaches 350°F.

- Spoon out a rounded tablespoon or so of the batter, scrape it into the oil using another spoon—remember, irregular is better—and fry until golden brown and cooked through, 2 to 3 minutes. Drain on a brown paper bag.

SPANISH COD FRITTERS

INSTRUCTIONS

- Transfer the cod to a medium saucepan, add the onion and bay leaf, cover with fresh water by 2 inches, and bring to a gentle simmer over medium-low heat. Cook the salt cod until it flakes easily when poked with a fork, 10 to 12 minutes.

- Using a slotted spoon, transfer the cod to a plate, leaving the onion and bay leaf in the pan, and set aside until the fish is cool enough to handle. Bring the water the salt cod was simmered to a boil, drop in the potato, and cook until tender, about 10 minutes. Drain in a colander. Toss the bay leaf, and keep the onion.

- Put the potato and onion into a bowl and mash them well. Remove any skin, bones, and miscellaneous bits and bobs from the cooled cod, then shred it. Stir the cod shreds, garlic, and parsley into the potato mixture. Set aside.

INGREDIENT

- 10 ounces salt cod soaked
- 1 small onion peeled and quartered
- 1 bay leaf
- 1 medium Yukon Gold potato diced
- 2 garlic cloves minced
- 2 tablespoons chopped flat-leaf parsley leaves
- Salt and freshly ground black pepper
- 3/4 cup water
- 1 tablespoon olive oil
- 1/4 cup all-purpose flour
- 2 large eggs
- Vegetable oil for frying

(See cooking instructions on page 98)

BRACIOLE - SICILIAN STYLE

INGREDIENTS FOR SIMPLE TOMATO SAUCE:

- 1 plus 1/2 Vidalia onion - finely minced
- 3/4 cup olive oil
- 1/4 tsp. red pepper flakes
- 4 large basil leaves
- 4 to 5 cans (28 ounces) Italian peeled tomatoes, blended in a blender
- 1/2 Tbsp. salt

- In a large heavy-bottomed pot, add the olive oil, onions, red pepper flakes, and basil, and simmer on medium-low heat for about 10 minutes. Then add only one can of tomatoes (blended) to the onions to prevent the onions from burning while cooking. (This is a trick my husband learned from his mom). Occasionally stirring. Continue to simmer the onions on low heat for another 15 minutes.

- Then add in the rest of the tomatoes and salt. Cover and raise the heat to bring the sauce to a boil. Lower the heat again, and continue to simmer the sauce on low heat.

- Add the braciole to the sauce. Simmer for an additional hour, occasionally stirring the sauce. The total cooking time should be about 1 and 1/2 hours. Taste the sauce. Turn off the heat. Allow the sauce to cool down slightly.

INGREDIENT

- 6 thinly sliced top sirloin steak (about 1/4-inch thick)
- 6 Tbsp. plain bread crumbs
- 4 to 6 Tbsp. grated pecorino cheese
- 4 ounces sliced prosciutto
- One 3-ounce wedge of provolone cheese- cut into 1/2-inch chunks
- 3 green onions, cleaned and cut to fit the width of the meat
- Fresh parsley
- Extra virgin olive oil, for sauteing the meat
- Salt and pepper

BRACIOLE - SICILIAN STYLE

My mom made braciole a recipe that originated in Prizzi and also one from her family in Campania. This is the Sicilian style recipe with thinly sliced top round sirloin steak, stuffed with cured meat, bread crumbs, cheese, and green onion, then rolled up and finished in a slow-cooked tomato sauce until the meat is perfectly tender.

INSTRUCTIONS

- On a clean surface working with 1 package of sliced steak at a time lay the slices flat on wax paper. Scatter bread crumbs over the steaks then again with grated pecorino cheese. Lightly drizzle olive oil over the cheese. Lay a slice or two of prosciutto on top, then in the center (or at the end of one side) add a chunk of provolone cheese, green onions, and a sprig of fresh parsley on top (which I forgot to add). Grab one end of the meat and roll tightly, then tie with a strong string, or butcher's twine to secure. You can also use strong toothpicks to secure the meat. Finally, sprinkle braciole with salt and pepper. Set them aside in a dish. Repeat with the other package of sliced steak.

- Place a large skillet on the stovetop and add a drizzle of olive oil. Heat the oil for a few seconds, add the braciole, and sear and braise the meats for a few minutes, rotating to brown evenly on all sides.

- Don't worry, it doesn't have to be fully cooked, the sauce will finish cooking the braciole.

- Transfer each one to the tomato sauce (recipe below) which should already be simmering and submerge each one into the sauce. Simmer the braciole for 1 hour, uncovered. Then cover with a lid, turn off the heat and allow it to sit and cool down slightly.

- Remove the braciole from the sauce. Using a sharp knife carefully remove the string and discard. Slice the braciole into thirds, and transfer to a serving platter. Ladle with extra sauce on top and serve.

SICILIAN CUISINE

Sicilian cuisine is very diverse, as it has been influenced by the many cultures that visited the island in ancient times. Couscous or cuscusu as it's called in Sicilian dialect is a very important example. Couscous is typically a traditional Moroccan dish, but while in the African coast it is prepared with meat and vegetables, in Sicily - and more precisely in Trapani - it is seasoned with fresh fish caught in the Mediterranean Sea.

Like most other dishes, recipes for Couscous. vary around the island. Learned to make couscous from world-renowned Chef Pino Maggiore, owner of Cantina Siciliana in Trapani. I first met Chef in 2012 at his restaurant in Trapani, where he taught me step-by-step how to make the fish broth and to use semolina wheat to prepare the couscous.
: I invited Chef Pinto to teach students at UAPTC- Culinary Arts & Hospitality Management Institute how to make the fish couscous. It was a great pleasure to work side-by-side with Chef Pino as we taught the students.
I assisted him while he taught the class. It was a great pleasure to work side-by-side with this great Chef and keep learning from him. These are the pictures of some of the students and a recipe to make Trapani Style Couscous. If you are in Trapani, Sicily, go enjoy a lesson or a meal with Chef Pino.

If you are in Trapani, Sicily, go enjoy a lesson or a meal with Chef Pino Maggiore at Cantina Siciliana.

TRAPANI STYLE COUSCOUS

SERVES 6-8

INGREDIENTS

- Prepare the fish broth
- 3 quarts water
- 1 cup dry white wine
- 3 cloves garlic skin removed and lightly smashed
- 1 0nion, root end removed, skin on and quartered
- 2 celery stalks, cleaned and cut in thirds
- 3 Roma tomatoes, stem side removed and halved
- 2 bay leaves
- 1 bunch parsley, cleaned
- 1 pinch saffron threads (optional)
- 5-10 peppercorns
- 1 tablespoon salt
- 4 lbs of mixed fish and shellfish. Such as sea bream, red snapper, scorpionfish, grouper, swordfish, mussels, clams, calamari rings, shrimp. Use a minimum of three to five different fish/shellfish combinations to give it the most complex and rich flavor.

BROTH PREPARATION:

- Fill a medium or large pot with 3 quarts of water. Add the white wine, garlic, onion, celery, tomatoes, bay leaves, parsley, saffron, peppercorns, and salt. Cover the pan and bring to a boil. Once boiled, reduce to a simmer and cook for about 10 minutes.

INSTRUCTIONS

- Cooking the shellfish and fish: The combination of fish and shellfish that you use is entirely up to you according to what you like and availability.

- First, bring the broth to a simmer. Add the clams and mussels to the broth. Once they open, quickly remove them with a slotted spoon, season with salt and freshly cracked black pepper, and reserve in a bowl to collect any juices that might accumulate (We'll add them later for flavor).

- Add the calamari rings to the simmering broth until just cooked. Do not overcook or they will become rubbery.

- Clean and devein the shrimp, leaving the tail ends attached. Add the shrimp shells to the broth. Then rinse the shrimp under cold running water to clean them.

- Now, add the shrimp to the broth, boil it, and then reduce to a simmer. As the shrimp begin to cook and turn slightly pink in color, remove and season and add them to a bowl.

INSTRUCTIONS

- Next, crack the five lobster tails open with a knife creating two pieces.

- Add the lobster tails to the pot and bring to almost a boil again and then reduce to a simmer. They will take a little longer to cook than the shrimp, but not much.

- Once the lobster meat has firmed up (about 5 min cooking time) it should easily pull out from its shell by using a fork or your fingers. If not, let it cook a little longer.

- When done, remove from the pot, season the flesh side, and set them aside with the other seafood.

TO COOK THE FISH:

Cut all fish into one- or two-inch pieces depending on the size you prefer. Add them to the broth and bring to a gentle simmer. Do not let the broth boil or the delicate fish will break apart and your plate presentation will not be as dramatic. As they are done, scoop the fish out and add to a plate, season with a little salt and freshly cracked black pepper, and reserve in a dish deep enough to collect any juices that will collect as the fish rests.

Strain the broth through a fine-mesh strainer. You may have to strain it twice to remove all particles left behind. This broth will be used to cook the couscous and to flavor the sauce (see recipe below).

TIP: Remember, DO NOT overcook shrimp. A little underdone is better than overcooked.

- Heat a frying pan or a skillet that is at least 2 1/2 inches deep. Add 2 tablespoons of olive oil, garlic, and onion slices to the pan. Now, add enough water and a pinch of salt just to cover the ingredients. Bring to a boil, then reduce to a simmer. Leave to cook, stirring frequently until all the water evaporates. (This traditional method will smellow the garlic and onion before sautéing.)

- At this stage, add the remaining 2 tablespoons of olive oil and cook for an additional 3 to 5 minutes until the onion and garlic become golden brown. Make sure you stir occasionally.

- Then, you can add tomatoes and almonds. Season with some salt and freshly cracked black pepper. Mash the tomatoes with the help of a fork while cooking.

- Add 2 cups of fish broth and keep cooking (about 15 – 20 minutes). Stirring occasionally, let it reduce to a nice sauce-like consistency.

- Remove the pan from the stove and season to taste. Measure out about 1/2 cup of the sauce and reserve. It will be added to the cooked couscous.

- You can now add all fish and shellfish to this sauce and cover with tin foil and/ or a lid.

INSTRUCTIONS

COOKING THE COUSCOUS

- 5 cups couscous
- 2 bay leaves
- Zest of 1 lemon, carefully grate the yellow portion of the skin leaving the pith behind.
- 1/2 bunch parsley, cleaned and finely chopped
- Cook 5 cups of couscous by substituting the liquid with the strained fish broth. If there is not enough broth, top it off with a little water.
- Add the bay leaves and lemon zest to the broth and follow the manufacturer's cooking procedures.
- Once your couscous is cooked stir in the 1/2 cup of the reserved sauce, and the parsley.
- Now you can plate your Couscous alla Trapanese and serve it!

TO SERVE:

- Spoon some couscous onto a serving plate. Top it with the fish, making sure all dishes have an equal distribution of fish and shellfish.
- Sprinkle the dish with some chopped parsley
- Serve the remaining sauce on the side with a few lemon wedges.
- Drizzle a light ribbon of Extra Virgin Olive Oil over the dishes and serve immediately.

My mother's family, both father and mother, moved from Caserta, Campania to the east coast of America in the early 1900s, settling in Pennsylvania and Ohio. They were not farmers like my father's family. Her parents eventually moved to California and later met my father's family.

My grandfather owned a pizzeria in Los Angeles. I learned about Campania recipes in the pizzeria. Some of my fondest memories are watching my Mother and Aunt Genevieve baking in the kitchen. It was truly magic.

RICETTE DI FAMIGLIA NAPOLITANO

STUFFED CABBAGE ROLLS

INGREDIENTS

- 8 savoy cabbage leaves removed from 1 large cabbage
- .5 lbs ground pork
- .5 lbs ground beef
- 1 egg
- ⅓ cup homemade Italian breadcrumbs or panko
- ⅓ cups parmesan , freshly grated
- 2 cloves garlic
- ¼ cup white wine
- 2 tbsp tomato paste
- 1 cup chicken stock
- Salt and pepper

INSTRUCTIONS

- Preheat the oven to (375F) and bring a large pot of salted water to a boil. Put the meat, egg, panko crumbs, grated parmesan,1 clove of minced garlic and a pinch of salt and pepper in a large bowl. Using your hands, mix everything together until thoroughly incorporated, set aside. If you haven't already, peel the largest leaves from the cabbage, being careful not to tear them.

- Blanch them in boiling water for 5 minutes until softened (you'll probably need to do this in batches or 2 or 3). Let them drain on kitchen paper then pat them as dry. Once dried, cut the large middle stalk from each leaf so you're left with two halves (discard the stalk).

- Place 1 heaped tablespoon of meat mixture on the widest part of the cabbage leaf then roll it up tucking in the sides then place in a baking dish. Repeat with the rest of the meat mixture and cabbage leaves. Set aside.

- To make the sauce, add ½ tablespoon of olive oil to a small saucepan, add 1 clove of finely chopped garlic and saute for 1 minute until fragrant. Add the white wine and simmer to reduce by half.

- Add the chicken stock and tomato paste, whisk together then simmer for 5 minutes. Pour over the stuffed cabbage rolls, cover with foil and bake in the oven for 35 minutes. Remove from the oven, uncover and let sit for 5 minutes before serving. Serve with freshly grated parmesan. Use the highest quality chicken stock (preferably homemade.) The sauce doesn't simmer for long so a great quality stock will add a ton of flavor. You can prep the whole dish (without adding the sauce) in advance and store in the fridge until you are ready to bake.

HOMEMADE ITALIAN SAUSAGES

INSTRUCTIONS

- Remove the meat and defrost for about an hour, partially frozen to grind. Grind the diced meat in a food processor for 30-60 seconds or a meat grinder. Next add the minced garlic, herbs, salt and pepper. Make sure to use fresh rosemary and chop it very fine. Pour over the red wine and mix everything until thoroughly combined using your hands. Cover with cling film and let the meat marinate for at least 30 minutes if possible. If you have a sausage maker sip your meat into casings.

- Without the casing, carefully wrap the meat in cling wrap and tighten both ends. Bring a pot of water to a boil and turn off the heat. Add the sausages to the hot water for around 30 seconds so they firm up and keep their shape. Place on a plate and cut the edges to remove from the cling film. You can now let them cool and place in the fridge until you are ready to cook them. Either fry them in a little olive oil in a large pan until browned on all sides or put them on the grill. Cook for around 10 minutes. Make sure to use high-quality pork meat with a good ratio of fat; I recommend pork shoulder. If you use venison, add fat back to the meat, or the sausage will be dry. Wrap the sausage meat tightly, so no water gets inside. You can prepare the sausages in advance and store them in the fridge or freezer.

INGREDIENTS

Special Equipment - Cling film (plastic wrap)

These sausages are made from ground pork or venison, fennel seeds, garlic, and red wine. Perfect to grill and serve with a side of pasta, greens or lentils.

- 2lbs pork shoulder or venison (or a mix of the two meats, diced and frozen
- 2 tbsp fennel seeds
- 4 cloves garlic (large) minced
- 1/2 cup red wine
- 4 sprigs rosemary fresh, finely chopped
- 3 tsp sea salt
- 1 tsp freshly ground pepper

HOMEMADE SAUSAGE SEASONING

The most common herbs found in Italian sausages are rosemary, oregano and fennel but there are a whole list of seasonings you could use:

- Chili flakes (dried or jarred)
- Nduja - a spicy Calabrian salami
- Marjoram - dried
- Sage - fresh finely chopped
- Parsley - fresh finely chopped
- Red wine - give a delicious rich flavor

SMALL BATCH BREAD CRUMBS

Equipment
Baking sheet - Rolling pin

INGREDIENTS

- 2 cups cubed or torn bread
- 3 tablespoons olive oil
- ⅛ teaspoon kosher salt
- ⅛ teaspoon dried herbs (dried herbs (dried basil, rosemary, herbs de Provence, or garlic powder work well)

INSTRUCTIONS

- Heat oven to 400° F. Place the bread in a medium sized bowl. Pour olive oil over the bread and add the salt and dried herbs. Mix well and taste one to see if it is seasoned to your liking, adjust salt and herbs as necessary.

- Spread the bread out on a small sheet pan. Bake for 8 to 10 minutes, until they are golden brown.

- Once the toasted bread has cooled, grind the bread in a food processor and pulse until the desired consistency is reached.

TIPS

- Make sure your bread is dry but not rock hard. Breadcrumbs can be made from just about any type of bread. In fact, I like to keep a bag in my freezer where I put scraps of bread until I have enough to make a small batch. Make gluten free breadcrumbs by using gluten free bread. Experiment with different dried herbs.

SAUSAGE AND BROCCOLI RABE
(Salsiccia e Friarielli)

INGREDIENTS

Italians love their greens. And with some dishes, bitter is better! This combination is absolutely one of my favorite dishes. You make the sausages with red pepper flakes added into the herb seasoning. And I like the sausages prepared in a pan for this dish.

- 2 bunches of broccoli rabe (or friarielli if you can get your hands on them!)
- 4 Italian sausages (hot or mild, depending on your tastes)
- 2 garlic cloves, peeled and left whole
- 3 tbsp extra virgin olive oil
- 1 tsp red pepper flakes
- Salt to taste
- Water for pre-cooking broccoli rabe

What is Friarielli?
The Romans call it broccoletti due to its resemblance to broccoli. In Naples, locals call it friarielli while further south in the region of Puglia people refer to it as cime di rapa. In the United States it is known as broccoli rabe.

INSTRUCTIONS

- Fill a large pot with water and bring to a boil over high heat. Clean the broccoli rabe, removing the thick stems but preserving the leaves and the broccoli florets. When water starts to boil, transfer the broccoli rabe to the pot and let boil for about 8 minutes. Strain

- Heat a large frying pan over medium-high heat with olive oil and garlic, when the garlic starts to sizzle place your sausages in the pan. Brown the sausages on all sides.

- Transfer the broccoli rabe to the pan with the sausages. Simmer over medium heat for at least 10 minutes or until the sausages are cooked through.

- Serve with peperoncino oil and crusty bread.

(POLLO ALLA CACCIATORA)
CHICKEN CACCIATORE

SERVING 4-6

INGREDIENTS

- 8 chicken thighs, skin on and bone in
- 1 large carrot, finely chopped
- 1 stick celery, finely chopped
- 1 onion, finely chopped
- 2 cloves garlic, finely chopped
- ½ cup pancetta or bacon
- ½ cup olives green or black
- 1 cup chicken stock low sodium
- 14.5 oz crushed tomatoes
- ½ cup white wine
- 1 large sprig rosemary
- 1 bay leaf
- 1 tbsp olive oil
- Salt and pepper to taste

This dish is like a stew and can be served with rice. You can also substitute the chicken for rabbit.

TIPS

- Chicken - Use free-range chicken if possible for best flavor.
- Tomatoes - Use the highest quality ingredients - crushed tomatoes are best for this recipe.
- Wine - You can use a dry red or white wine to make this recipe. If you don't want to cook with wine then you can replace it with extra stock.
- Storage - leftovers will keep well in the fridge for 2-3 days and can be reheated. You can also freeze leftovers, thaw completely then reheat as needed.

INSTRUCTIONS

- Heat olive oil in a large deep sided skillet until hot. Sprinkle the chicken with salt then brown the chicken skin side down for 5-7 minutes until golden. Turn the chicken around and brown on the other side for 2 minutes then remove and set aside on a plate. Drain the excess fat from the skillet but don't wipe it clean.

- Add the pancetta to the hot skillet and fry for 2-3 minutes. Next add the finely chopped carrot, celery and onion and saute until soft but not browned around 5 minutes.

- Once soft, add the garlic, rosemary and bay and saute for another 2 minutes. Add the white wine and simmer for 1-2 minutes or until you can no longer smell the alcohol.

- Add the tomatoes and stock and stir everything together. Finally, add the chicken back to the pot, cover and simmer for 45 minutes.

- Uncover add the olives and simmer for a further 10 minutes to reduce the sauce slightly. While the sauce is reducing you can remove the chicken to a tray and place under a broiler (oven-grill) for a couple of minutes to crisp the skin up, this is optional but gives you delicious crispy skin. Add the chicken back in and serve.

Genovese Sauce
La Genovese Napoletana

SERVES: 6 - 8

This sauce is incredibly delicious! I learned it when I lived with a family on a farm in San Mauro Cilento. It simmers slowly in onions, beef and white wine.

INGREDIENTS

- 4 large yellow onions, finely sliced
- 2 carrots, finely chopped
- 2 celery stalks, finely chopped
- 1.3 lbs beef chuck roast cut into medium-large chunks
- ½ cup white wine or chicken stock
- 1 bay leaf
- ½ cup fresh parsley, roughly chopped
- 1-2 tbsp olive oil
- Salt and pepper for seasoning
- freshly grated parmesan, for serving

INSTRUCTIONS

- Prepare all the vegetables and sprinkle the beef with salt and pepper. Add the olive oil to a large pot on medium-low heat and add the onions, carrot and celery. Saute the onions for 10 minutes then add the beef, bay, and parsley.

- Let the beef brown on all sides, you'll need to stir the mixture around slightly so the beef touches the bottom of the pot. Cover the pot and let it slowly cook for 3 hours, stirring every now and then to make sure it doesn't stick.

- After 3 hours, remove the lid and add the white wine. Continue to simmer the ragu on medium-low heat for another hour.

- Once done taste and add more salt to taste then toss with cooked and drained pasta.

Sunday Supper Roast Chicken

SERVES: 6 - 8

This meal is soul food to me. It is so easy to make this one-pot meal that bastes itself and comes out extra juicy and full of flavor.

INGREDIENTS

- 2-3 lbs whole chicken, roasting hen preferred
- 1 whole lemon
- 2-3 cloves garlic, whole
- 1 tbsp dried oregano
- 1 tbsp dried rosemary
- 1 tbsp dried thyme
- 1 tbsp fennel seeds
- 1 tsp red pepper flakes
- 1 tablespoon sea salt flakes, plus extra for seasoning inside
- 1 tbsp olive oil

ADDITIONAL

- Roast the chicken for 1 hour for 2 lbs. Use a meat thermometer to test. It should read 165 degrees. If you don't have a thermometer, use a paring knife to make a small cut into the thigh going all the way to the bone. If you see any red flesh, put the bird back into the oven.

- Preheating the oven seems obvious but it's essential for making the perfect roast chicken. Pat the skin dry with paper towels first. Removing the moisture from the skin helps make it extra crispy.

- Rest the chicken after roasting or all the juices will run right out of the chicken.

INSTRUCTIONS

- Preheat the oven to 180 F and pierce the whole lemon all over with the tip of a sharp knife, set aside. Pat the chicken dry on all sides with kitchen paper. Season the cavity of the chicken well with salt then add two garlic cloves and a whole pierced lemon.

- Add the dried herbs, sea salt and red pepper flakes over the chicken and drizzle over the olive oil, rub all over the chicken. Turn it upside down on a baking tray and place in the preheated oven.

- Roast for 45 minutes then remove from the oven and turn the chicken around. Roast for another 45 minutes, the skin should be nice and crispy. Remove from the oven and let the chicken rest for 20-30 minutes. Enjoy.

Mangiamo

Coniglio all' Ischitana

SERVES: 6 - 8

INGREDIENTS

- 1 rabbit, (approx 3 pounds, cut into several large pieces)
- 1 ½ cup crushed tomatoes
- ½ cup white wine
- 3 garlic clove
- herbs, (thyme, marjoram, sage and rosemary)
- 1 tsp red pepper chilli flakes
- extra virgin olive oil
- salt, to taste

ADDITIONAL

Special Equipment
A terracotta pan or Dutch oven

INSTRUCTIONS

- Heat olive oil in a large heavy-bottomed terracotta pan or Dutch oven over medium-high heat. Once the oil is hot enough, place the entire garlic head in along with the chilli.

- Once garlic and chilli are golden/brown, then add the rabbit pieces making sure to get a nice sear on both sides.

- Next add the white wine along with the herbs and let it cook for about 2 minutes.

- Lastly, add the tomatoes and salt, and cover your pan with the lid for about 20 minutes.

- Remove the lid and let it continue to cook until the tomato sauce reduces and thickens up a bit. Remove from heat, salt to taste, and serve.

Steak Pizzaiola

SERVES: 6 - 8

We vacationed in a villa in Ischia one summer. They served the best rabbit I had ever tasted. It was cooked in a terracotta pan. Of course, I had to learn the recipe before I left the island. I have added my own personal touch to this dish, but it still melts in your mouth.

INGREDIENTS

- 4 steaks (I used thin-cut sirloin, but my Mom used a London broil cut into thin pieces)
- 1 tbsp olive oil
- 2 cloves garlic finely chopped
- 2 cups cherry tomatoes sliced in half
- ½ cup green olives
- 1 tsp capers
- 1 cup vegetable or chicken stock
- ⅓ cup white wine
- 1 tsp dried oregano
- 1 tbsp tomato paste
- 4-5 basil leaves for serving

ADDITIONAL

You can use any steak you like for this recipe just make sure they are quick-cooked steaks and not stewing beef. You can swap the steak for chicken or pork just make sure to cook it all the way through at the first stage of cooking and warm up in the sauce at the end.

Steak Cooking Time
For Thick Cut Steaks (1 inch)
Rare: ~ 1 and a half minutes each side
Medium rare: ~ 2 minutes each side
Medium: ~ 2 and a half minutes each side
Well done: 4 minutes each side

INSTRUCTIONS

- Heat the olive oil in a large skillet. Once hot, cook the steaks to your preference. (see notes below for cooking times) For 1 inch thick steaks I cook them for 1 minute each side. They will use more when added into the sauce. Once cooked, set the steaks aside on a plate.

- Turn the heat down to medium-low and add an extra drizzle of olive oil. Add the chopped garlic and fry for a few seconds until fragrant. Next, add the wine to deglaze the pan and scape/loosen any brown bits with a wooden spoon. Simmer for 1 minute.

- Add the cherry tomatoes and simmer until the skin starts to wrinkle (about 5 minutes). Add the olives, capers, tomato paste, oregano and stock, stir to combine everything and bring to a simmer. Simmer the tomato sauce gently for 10 minutes.

- Add the steaks back to the skillet with the sauce and cook until warmed through, serve garnished with some fresh basil.

STEAK TIPS

You can use any steak you like for this recipe just make sure they are quick-cooked steaks and not stewing beef. You can swap the steak for chicken or pork just make sure to cook it all the way through at the first stage of cooking and warm up in the sauce at the end.

Steak Cooking Time
For Thick Cut Steaks (1 inch)
Rare: ~ 1 and a half minutes each side
Medium rare: ~ 2 minutes each side
Medium: ~ 2 and a half minutes each side
Well done: 4 minutes each side

NEAPOLITAN BRACIOLE

My momma didn't make traditional Neapolitan braciole. She added thinly sliced celery and prosciutto to the otherwise classic ingredients of pine nuts, raisons, cheese and parsley. Then simply simmered in tomato sauce until tender. I still make it this way because I like the extra flavor and texture these two ingredients add.

What kind of meat is best for Braciole?

Top round sirloin steak works well for Italian beef braciole. Sandwich steaks are a more economical option. Some people prefer to use bottom round beef roast or flank steak. You will need thin slices so it's easiest to head to a butcher and get him to cut it thin and even for you. You'll need to get ¼-inch slices so they're thick enough not to fall apart yet thin enough to enclose the filling and cook until tender.

Neapolitan Braciole

SERVES: 4

INGREDIENTS

- 4 slices of Top Round Sirloin Steak
- 2 ounces of pine nuts
- 1.5 ounces of sultanas
- 3 ounces of pecorino cheese
- 12 ounces of tomato sauce
- 1 clove of garlic
- Parsley
- 1 stalk celery, thinly sliced
- 4 slices of prosciutto, thinly sliced
- 1/2 onion
- 1/2 glass of white wine
- basil
- salt
- pepper
- extra virgin olive oil

INSTRUCTIONS

- Place the slices of meat on a cutting board and beat them lightly with a meat mallet. Sprinkle the slices of meat with salt and pepper, prosciutto, then add a handful of pine nuts, celery and raisins. Add the garlic and chopped parsley and finally cover everything with the pecorino, leaving the edges of the meat free. Close the slices by rolling them up like a roll and wrap them with string.

- In a large saucepan, fry the onion in a couple of tablespoons of oil. Place the chops in the pan and brown them. Deglaze with the white wine.

- Now add the tomato puree and basil and cover with a lid. Cook the chops in the sauce over a very low heat for at least two hours or until tender.

THE ITALIAN MEATBALL

Believe it or not, the meatballs we know and love today didn't originate in Italy. Although meatballs cooked in tomato sauce and served with pasta is likely what most Americans imagine, it is virtually impossible to find it served this way in Italy.

Meatballs are most often a stand-alone dish—enjoyed as a snack or served as a second course without any sauce or with a light soup broth. They can be fried, steamed or baked in the oven with a drizzle of olive oil. Traditional Italian meatballs typically contain equal portions of meat and soaked bread, and other additions such as eggs, garlic, parsley, vegetables and cheese. They may be made with beef, lamb, turkey, or even fish, depending on what meat is available.

I make meatballs every week for my market with freshly ground pork and beef. After years of working on my recipe, I love my classic recipe. It starts with a panade to keep the meatball moist and tender.

LEARNING

TECHNIQUES

How to prepare

Panade

A panade is a mixture of starch and liquid that is added to ground meat. Any combination of starch (bread, panko, crackers) and liquids (milk, buttermilk, yogurt, stock, water) can be used.

INGREDIENTS

- 1 cup bread, cut into ½-inch cubes
- 1 cup milk, plus more as needed to cover bread

INSTRUCTIONS

- Place bread into a medium-sized bowl and then pour 1 cup of milk or more as needed to cover the bread.

- Allow bread cubes to soak for at least 10 minutes until most of the milk has absorbed and the bread is mushy in texture.

- Pour off any excess milk and mash the bread mixture with a fork until there are no dry spots. The mixture should look like a starchy paste.

SERVES 12
MARGIE'S MEATBALLS

INGREDIENTS

- 1 ½ lbs ground beef either 80/20 or 85/15 ,grass-fed if possible
- ½ lb ground pork
- 1 yellow onion roughly chopped
- 3 cloves garlic peeled, smashed
- ¼ cup fresh basil leaves
- ¼ cup fresh parsley leaves Italian, flat leaf
- Panade
- 1 egg
- ½ cup parmesan cheese, good quality and fresh grated
- 1½ tsp kosher salt
- ½ tsp black pepper
- ½ tsp red pepper flakes

INSTRUCTIONS

- Use a food processor to finely chop herbs and aromatics. Add onion, garlic, basil and parsley, close and turn on for 30 seconds. Open and scrape down sides, return cover and blend for another 15 seconds. Be careful not to over-process and liquefy. Set Aside.

- Season the panade (recipe above) with parmesan cheese, egg, salt, black pepper and red pepper. Mix thoroughly. Add ground beef and pork, using a fork to break the meat apart as you add to the bowl. Use a fork to gently incorporate all ingredients together. It will be almost like a scraping and fluffing motion. You don't want to over mix meat, as it will become tough. Then use your hands to continue to thoroughly combine.

- Roll the meatball into whatever size you prefer. I made large ones, but if I were making for soup or for grinders or appetizers I would have made them smaller. Evenly space onto a baking sheet lined with parchment paper. Place in a preheated oven on the upper rack to get a nice sear on top. Bake for about 15-20 minutes. Time depends on the size of the meatballs. Remove from the oven and let simmer with tomato for 20 minutes. Serve as an appetizer or main course.

Preparing this section of the cookbook conjured up fond memories of my mother baking in the kitchen. She was a great cook but baking was her true gift. On weekdays, our dessert was fruit and a biscotti or cookie except in the summer when we enjoyed granita and gelati. The holidays brought the magic - my mother, aunts, and nonna laughing and chatting in a small kitchen while they baked the zeppola, pignolata, ricotta cheesecake, and other special sweets.

The recipes in this section are from our family in Sicily and Naples. I hope they bring you as much joy in your tummy and heart as they do me. When you bake them, think about these Italian ladies laughing as they bake.

Or better yet, make your own sweet noise.

DOLCI

6

Campania, Italy

Sicily, Italy

THE STORY
Behind My Recipe

If you've eaten dessert in Italy or at an Italian American home, you know that our sweets are not too sweet. Sugar was too expensive for most families in the past, so age-old family recipes include natural sweetening agents, such as fruit and honey. Italian dessert recipes are broken down into two groups. The ancient or the oldest of the sweets that were derived from bread recipes. A little honey or fruit was added to sweeten bread recipes. Torrone dates back to Roman times when it was used in religious ceremonies. This nougat confection is made with egg whites, nuts, and honey and is popular all over the Mediterranean. Later came the more modern recipes like Italian cheesecake, Panna Cotta, Cannoli, and Italian cream puffs, when sugar, milk, eggs, honey, and almonds became plentiful.

Families that immigrated to America, like mine, changed the classic desserts because some of the ingredients were unavailable. For example, ricotta cheese was substituted for hard-to-find mascarpone cheese in desserts such as cannoli and cheesecake. Like all countries, Italy has its own Italian food customs for holidays and special occasions like Easter and Christmas.

Sicily, Italy

SICILIAN KNOT COOKIES

The Sicilian knot cookie is the first cookie recipe I learned how to make from my mom and nonna. To this day, these cookies bring back so many childhood memories. We ate these cookies for breakfast, dunked in coffee or milk. They were always on the holiday cookie tray and just perfect with a cup of gelato! My nonna told us the "S-shape" stood for Sicilian. I still believe it as an adult even though I have no evidence of its truth!

INGREDIENT

- 4 1/2 cups all-purpose flour
- 2 teaspoons baking powder
- 4 eggs additional 1 for egg wash
- 1 cup granulated sugar plus extra for topping
- 3/4 cup vegetable oil
- Zest of one lemon or orange
- 1 teaspoon of pure vanilla extract
- Note: You can substitute the vanilla for anise or almond extract.

INSTRUCTIONS

- Preheat the oven to 375 degrees. Prepare several baking sheets by lining them with parchment paper and set aside.

- In a large bowl, whisk together the flour and baking powder; set aside. Add eggs, sugar, oil and lemon zest to your mixer bowl. Mix on low speed until combined.

- Slowly add in the flour, mix 1/2 cup portion at a time and mix on medium speed until you have a soft dough. Take care not to over mix the dough. Dump out the dough onto a clean and lightly floured surface. Work the dough just a bit until it is smooth and cohesive. Scoop out portions (2 Tablespoons) of the dough in place on the floured surface.

- How to Shape "S or Knot" CookiesScoop out portions (2 Tablespoons) of the dough on the floured surface. Roll the dough piece into a 4-5 inch strand (1/2 inch diameter). Form into an S and place on a parchment lined baking sheet. You could pull portions of dough and they could be between 3-8 inches long. It tastes equally delicious if it looks like a snake! Press gently to flatten a little. Continue shaping the rest of the cookies and place them about 1-inch apart.

- In a small bowl beat the egg to make the egg wash. Brush each cookie with the egg wash. Bake for 15-20 minutes and until golden brown. Depending on the size, some could be done sooner, so be sure to start checking them at about 13 minutes.

- Let cool completely before storing. Store at room temperature in an airtight container. Alternatively, place them in a zipped lock freezer bag (be sure all the air is squeezed out of it)or in an airtight container for up to 3 months. Defrost at room temperature before serving.

PANAFORTE

INGREDIENTS

- 1 cup whole hazelnuts
- 1 cup blanched almonds
- 1 cup coarsely chopped candied orange peel
- 1 cup finely chopped citron
- 1 teaspoon grated lemon zest
- ½ cup unbleached all-purpose flour
- 1 teaspoon ground cinnamon
- ¼ teaspoon ground coriander
- ¼ teaspoon ground cloves
- ¼ teaspoon freshly ground nutmeg
- Pinch ground white pepper
- ¾ cup granulated sugar
- ¾ cup honey
- 2 tablespoons unsalted butter
- Confectioners' sugar

INSTRUCTIONS
SERVES 8

- Heat oven to 350 degrees. Toast hazelnuts on a baking sheet in the oven until the skins pop and blister, 10 to 15 minutes. Rub the skins from the hazelnuts in a kitchen towel. Toast the almonds on a baking sheet until very pale golden, about 10 to 15 minutes. Chop the almonds and hazelnuts very coarsely. Reduce oven temperature to 300 degrees.

- Mix the nuts, orange peel, citron, lemon zest, flour, cinnamon, coriander, cloves, nutmeg and pepper together thoroughly in a large mixing bowl.

- Butter a nine-inch springform pan, line the bottom and sides with parchment paper and then butter the paper. Heat the granulated sugar, honey and butter in a heavy saucepan over low heat, stirring constantly until the syrup registers 242 to 248 degrees on a candy thermometer (a little of the mixture will form a ball when dropped into cold water). Immediately pour the syrup into the mixture and stir quickly until thoroughly blended. Pour immediately into the prepared pan and smooth the top with a spatula. The batter will become stiff and sticky very quickly so you must work fast.

- Bake for about 40 minutes. The panforte won't color or seem very firm even when ready but it will harden as it cools. Cool on a rack until the cake is firm to the touch. Remove the sides of the pan and invert the cake onto a sheet of waxed paper. Peel off the parchment paper. Dust heavily with confectioners' sugar.

- **NOTES**
Storage: Panforte can be kept for several months, well wrapped, at room temperature

CLASSIC ITALIAN PIZZELLE COOKIES

Pizzelles in Italian basically means small rounds. Pizze means round or flat and is the same root word that pizza comes from. This pizzelle recipe makes a classic Italian pizzelle with anise and is lightly sweet and crisp. Anise oil has a very strong licorice flavor. If you use too much, it can overpower the entire pizzelle.

Pizzelle dough is very thick and sticky. When you scoop it up with a spoon, it will stick to the spoon so you will have to push it off with your finger or another spoon to get it on to the pizzelle maker.
To make the pizzelles, you need a special pizzelle maker. It looks like a small waffle iron but the grooves on it are very shallow. You can shape the pizzelle to make homemade ice cream cones and faux cannoli shells.

INGREDIENTS

- 3 eggs
- ¾ cup of sugar
- 1 ¾ cups of all purpose flour
- 2 teaspoon of baking powder
- 1 ½ teaspoon of vanilla
- 3 tiny drops of anise to do this, pour a tiny amount of anise on to a spoon. Slowly turn the spoon downward over your mixture and wait for 3 tiny drops to fall and then you are done!
- 1 stick 8 tablespoon melted unsalted butter
- ¼ teaspoon kosher salt

ADDITIONAL

- If you prefer, you can substitute vanilla, almond or lemon extract or add chocolate.

- To make chocolate pizzelles: Use 1 ½ cups of flour plus 2 tablespoons. Add ¼ cup of cocoa powder (good quality) to the flour before adding the wet ingredients.

- For the sugar, increase the amount of sugar in the recipe by ¼ cup (for a total of 1 cup of sugar in the recipe).

- To make Vanilla pizzelles: Omit the anise and add an extra ½ teaspoon of vanilla extract.

- To make lemon pizzelles: Omit the anise and vanilla and add ½ teaspoon of lemon extract.

- To make almond pizzelles: Omit the anise extract and ¼ teaspoon of almond extract.

INSTRUCTIONS

- Whisk together your eggs, sugar, vanilla and anise (see how to anise above) in a medium bowl. Now add your flour, salt and baking powder and mix it well until there are no lumps and it looks smooth. Now add your melted butter and mix that into your mixture.

- Preheat your pizzelle maker. They are all a little different so follow the manufacturer's instructions for this. Once it is heated, add a heaping tablespoon of your thick dough to the middle of each of your pizzelle areas on the iron. Close and cook for about 30-45 seconds until it is a light golden color. If the pizzelle is too light in color you can just close the pizzelle maker and cook the pizzelle for a few more seconds.

- Once they are cooked, remove the pizzelles from the iron (they will still be soft and pliable at this point) and place on a cooling rack where they will cool and get nice and crispy. If you want to shape them into a roll, cone or cup, now is the time. Keep doing this until all the dough is used up!

Storing Pizzelles

Pizzelles store very well in the freezer. I know this well because my Aunt Vivian always has a container of her Anise Pizzelles in her freezer! Once they cool completely, please put them in an airtight container for short-term storage. If you want to keep them fresh for up to 2 months, place them in a freezer-proof container.

LEARNING TECHNIQUES
How to prepare
Sicilian Fig Cookie Dough

Sicilian Fig Cookies, Cucidati, are said to have originated hundreds of years ago in Sicily, particularly in the Palermo region, where there is a strong Arab influence. They are deliciously moist, tender, and sweet fruit- and nut-filled cookies. The filling generally consists of some combination of walnuts, dates, figs, honey, spices and orange – all of which were first introduced by the Arabic people who lived on the island.

PREPARING THE FILLING

- Making the filling

- Remove the tough stem from the figs then chop them into roughly quarters. Roughly chop the dates, if not already chopped.

- Place the figs, dates, raisins, almonds, chocolate, honey, marmalade/jam, brandy/whisky and cinnamon in the food processor and blend until a relatively smooth paste forms, scraping down and pulsing slightly more as needed.

PREPARING COOKIE DOUGH

- Put the flour, sugar, baking powder and salt in a food processor and pulse briefly to mix. Add the butter, in small cubes, the vanilla and egg and pulse to form crumbs. Add the milk and pulse a couple times to bring the mixture together.

- Remove the blade from the food processor and take out the dough. Knead it briefly (just once or twice) and bring the dough together in a ball. Wrap it in cling wrap/film and chill for at least an hour or two until firm or leave overnight. If you leave overnight, you may need to take it out 20 min or so before rolling so it is not too cold.

SICILIAN FIG COOKIES

GLAZE

- ¼ cup confectioner's sugar
- ½ tablespoon lemon juice
- 1 tablespoon small round sprinkles

INGREDIENTS | INSTRUCTIONS

FOR COOKIE DOUGH

- 1 cup all purpose flour
- 3 tablespoon sugar
- ¼ teaspoon baking powder
- ¼ teaspoon salt
- 2 oz unsalted butter (½ stick)
- ¼ teaspoon vanilla extract
- 1 egg
- 1 tablespoon milk

FOR FILLING

- ½ cup dried figs
- ¼ cup dates
- ¼ cup raisins
- 2 tablespoons blanched almonds
- 1 tablespoon chocolate chips
- 1 ½ tablespoon honey
- 2 tablespoon marmalade or apricot preserves
- 1 tablespoon brandy or whiskey, marsala
- ¼ teaspoon cinnamon

TIPS FOR MAKING THESE COOKIES

- Make the pastry ahead of time and chill it until it firms up.
- Let the food processor chop and mix
- (Remember to trim the tips off the figs).
- Make smaller rather than a big long roll to make things easier.
- Wait until the cookies are completely cool before adding glaze.

Mangiamo | 133

LEARNING TECHNIQUES

How to prepare Sicilian Fig Cookie Dough

Sicilian Fig Cookies, Cucidati, are said to have originated hundreds of years ago in Sicily, particularly in the Palermo region, where there is a strong Arab influence. They are deliciously moist, tender, and sweet fruit- and nut-filled cookies. The filling generally consists of some combination of walnuts, dates, figs, honey, spices and orange – all of which were first introduced by the Arabic people who lived on the island.

FORMING AND BAKING COOKIES

- Preheat the oven to 350F/175C. Line a baking sheet/tray with parchment or a silicone mat. Unwrap the cookie dough and roll it on a floured surface into roughly 10in x 8in (25cm x 20cm) rectangle. Neaten off the edges, so they are relatively straight.

- Cut the piece of dough in half the long way (i.e., so you have two pieces around 10 x 4in). Separate the pieces of dough slightly to make them easier to work with and ensure they are not stuck to the work surface. Divide the filling in two and use half to make a log the length of one of the pieces of dough in the middle. Make sure it goes right to the end. Roll over one side of the dough and keep rolling so it goes all the way rough and the join is on the bottom. It is fine if it overlaps slightly. Cut the log into slices roughly 1 -1 ½ in length. Transfer them to the lined baking sheet and then repeat with the rest of the dough and filling.

- Bake the cookies for approximately 15 minutes until the dough looks slightly dry and just begins to brown at the edges and underneath. They may feel slightly soft on top, but they should feel dry. Allow to cool a couple of minutes, then transfer to a cooling rack to cool completely.

- Once the cookies have completely cooled, Place the cooling rack with the cookies over a baking sheet (to collect any dropped sprinkles).

- Sift the confectioner's sugar into a small bowl. Add the lemon juice and mix until smooth. Drizzle/spoon a little of the glaze on top of around 3-4 cookies at a time, then sprinkle some sprinkles on top. Repeat with the rest. Allow the glaze to dry before transferring it to a container. The cookies will keep well for a good few days or more, the sprinkles may just bleed a little color.

SFINCI DI SAN GIUSEPPE

Always held on March 19th, the Feast of St. Joseph honors Virgin Mary's husband, Joseph, and earthly father to Jesus. It is also the day in which Italy celebrates Father's Day. The feast is prominent in Southern Italy, particularly Sicily, where he is the Patron Saint. Sfingi, Cannoli, and Zeppole are traditional Italian pastries served each March 19 for St Joseph's Day. Sfingi - fried pieces of bread dough served in a brown paper bag loaded with sugar. Nothing reminds me more of my bisnonna than the smell of yeasty bread frying, the sound of the sfingi and sugar shaking in the bag.

INGREDIENTS

SERVES 24

- 1 cup sugar + ¼ cup sugar
- 1 teaspoon cinnamon
- 4 cups all-purpose flour
- 1 teaspoon baking powder
- 1 teaspoon Kosher Salt
- 2 tablespoons dry active yeast
- 1 tablespoon pure vanilla extract
- 2 cups warm water 110-113 degrees
- Canola oil for frying

INSTRUCTIONS

- Mix flour, baking powder, and salt in a bowl and whisk to combine. Set aside. In a large bowl or cup with a pouring lip, add yeast and ¼ cup sugar to warm water and stir to dissolve. Add the vanilla and stir to combine. Let the yeast bloom for 5 minutes.

- In a stand mixer, pour the yeast mixture into the mixer bowl. Using the whisk attachment, gradually add the flour mixture until a shaggy dough is formed. Switch to the dough hook and knead for 5 - 7 minutes until a smooth ball is formed. Dough should be slightly sticky and elastic. Put the dough into an oiled bowl, cover it with plastic wrap and let rise in a warm place until doubled in size, about 1 ½ hours. Punch down, cover, and let it rise again for 30 minutes.

- Transfer the dough to a floured board. Divide into 4 pieces. Working with one piece at a time, pinch or cut small pieces about the size of a lime. With floured hands, roll into balls. Place on parchment paper dusted with flour. Repeat with the rest of the dough. You should get about 24 balls.

- Combine the 1 cup sugar and cinnamon in a shallow bowl. Set aside. To fry, heat oil to 350 degrees in a skillet on the stovetop deep enough to submerge the sfinge, or in an electric deep fryer (my preference). Carefully drop about 6 balls at a time in the hot oil. Fry for about 3-5 minutes golden brown. If the balls don't roll over independently, you must flip them with a fork. Drain on paper towels. While still warm, roll the sfingi in cinnamon sugar. Enjoy right away. They are best eaten warm.

ZEPPOLA
SERVES 10

INGREDIENTS

VANILLA EGG CUSTARD FILLING

- 3 cups Half & Half whole milk and cream
- 8 large egg yolks let eggs come to room temperature before cooking
- ½ cup superfine sugar
- ¼ cup cornstarch
- ¼ teaspoon salt
- 1 tablespoon butter softened to room temperature
- 1 teaspoon vanilla extract
- 1 whole vanilla seed pod

INGREDIENTS

PATE CHOUX PASTRY DOUGH

- 1 cup water or milk
- ½ cup 1 stick butter, cut in 4 pieces
- ½ teaspoon salt
- 1 cup bread flour
- 5 large eggs
- Garnish
- 10 sweet maraschino cherries drained
- ¼ cup powdered sugar

INSTRUCTIONS

- Heat milk in a saucepan over medium heat until very hot. Watch closely and do not let it boil. In the meantime, using an electric hand beater, whisk together yolks, sugar, cornstarch, and salt in a large glass bowl (or other heatproof-type of bowl) until smooth

- Add 1 cup hot milk to the yolk mixture in a stream, whisking by hand or by an electric beater to incorporate. Repeat with the rest of the hot milk, whisking constantly. Transfer mixture to the saucepan and cook over moderately low heat, stirring constantly, until thickened and registers 160°F on thermometer, or approximately 6 to 10 minutes. (Do not go over 165 degrees F or the eggs will start to scramble). Add more half & half if the custard is too thick.

- Watch closely and do not let it boil. Remove the pan from the stove and let the custard cool for 10 minutes. Using a ladle, transfer the custard, one ladle at a time, through a fine-mesh sieve into a clean bowl. Use the back of the ladle or a spatula to push it through as needed. Repeat until all the custard is strained.

- Stir in butter and vanilla extract. Split the vanilla pod with a sharp knife and scrape the seeds into the custard. Stir until the vanilla seeds are evenly mixed in the custard. Cover the surface of the custard with wax paper and chill in the refrigerator until cold and thickened, at least 3 hours. The custard is best chilled overnight in the fridge.

FOR PATE CHOUX ZEPPOLE

- Preheat the oven to 425 degrees. Line two baking sheets with parchment paper. With a pencil, trace 10 3-inch circles onto parchment paper. Turn the parchment over. The stencil will show through.

- Combine water (or milk), butter and salt in a large saucepan on the stovetop over medium high heat. Bring to a rolling boil, whisking several times to combine the butter and milk.

- When boiling, add flour all at one time, and stir with a stiff spoon. Keep stirring until the dough forms a ball and looks smooth. Transfer the dough to a Kitchenaid bowl.

- With the paddle, mix the dough to cool until it reaches under 140 degrees. Note: eggs will scramble at 165 degrees so knowing the temperature is important. Use a digital thermometer to check the temperature. To speed up the cooling process, slide an ice pack underneath the Kitchenaid bowl.

- When the temperature is 140 degrees or less, add one egg at a time, fully incorporating the egg before adding the next. Continue mixing until the dough is thick and smooth, and soft peaks form.

- Transfer the pate choux dough to a pastry bag fitted with a large open star border tip or a Wilton 1M. Pipe out Zeppoles following the stencils on parchment paper. Optional to shape like a donut or giant cream puff. If any pointy tips are created from the piping, pat down with a wet finger.

- Bake for 20 minutes or until puffed up and golden.

- Remove the Zeppole from the oven and let cool on a wire rack. The steam from the center will escape and the inside will dry out. Fill another pastry bag fitted with a large star tip with the cold

TIP: VANILLA EGG CUSTARD

- If shaped like cream puffs: With a small knife cut a cross in the bottom of the Zeppole. Insert the tip into a cross mark and pipe the custard to fill the hollow center of each one.

- If shaped like donuts: When the zeppole have cooled completely, cut them in half. Generously pipe the filling on the cut half. Cover with the top half. Garnish the Zeppole with a dusting of powdered sugar, pipe one dollop of filling on top and garnish top with a maraschino cherry. Serve immediately.

- Unfilled Zeppoles can be stored in an airtight container in the fridge for a few days or frozen for later use.

SICILIAN CANNOLI

INGREDIENTS

- 2 cups flour
- 1 tablespoon bitter cocoa powder
- 4 tablespoon confectioners sugar
- 4 tablespoon lard optional
- 1 pinch salt
- 1 teaspoon cinnamon powder
- 1 teaspoon instant coffee
- 1 egg
- 1 oz white wine vinegar
- 1 oz Marsala wine

CANNOLI FILLING
- 3 cups ricotta cheese
- 1/2 cup dark chocolate drops
- 1.5 cups sugar
- Garnish
- 24 Candied cherries
- Powdered sugar as required

INSTRUCTIONS

- Before you begin to prepare the cannoli shells (called "scorcie"), put the cheese to drain in a colander placed in a bowl, then store it in the fridge. Put in a large mixing bowl the flour, salt, cinnamon, powdered coffee, cocoa and sift the confectioners sugar. Add the lard, egg, and then the vinegar mixed with Marsala wine; the latter liquids should be added slowly, kneading the composition every time, as depending on how much the flour absorbs, you might not need to add the entire Marsala and vinegar mix. Keep in mind that the dough should be soft and elastic but firm.

- Knead the mixture for 5 minutes on a work surface, until it is elastic, smooth and homogeneous, then wrap it in plastic and leave it to rest for at least an hour in the refrigerator. Now to prepare the cannoli cream for the topping, you will need to take the well-drained ricotta cheese and place it inside a bowl where you add sugar. Gently stir the ingredients without applying too much pressure, then cover the bowl with plastic wrap and place in the refrigerator for at least an hour. After the indicated time, take a very fine mesh sieve, place it on a bowl and with the help of a spatula, crush the ricotta and sugar down and press on it, so that what comes out through the sieve is a very fine cream.

RECIPE

- Once the composition has the right density, add the chocolate chips (or, if you prefer, candied pumpkin cubes). Mix and place the cream cheese in the refrigerator, inside a container with a lid. Take the dough for the cannoli shells and place it on the table. Use a rolling pin to create a thin 1-2 mm pastry. Use round pastry rings to create at least 24 pieces. Stretch the 24 circles, then roll them around cannoli molds (if you have metal cylinders that work too), brushing the ends with the whites before stacking them.

- Heat the lard (or oil) in a saucepan not too big, until you get to 170-180 °C (338-356 F) and then fry all the cannoli shells. Place them afterwards on a couple of sheets of absorbent paper, to get rid of the extra oil, and let them cool completely before removing the metal cylinders. Once they have cooled, fill the cannoli shells with the cannoli cream that you will put in a pastry bag, using a smooth and wide nozzle. Complete the process by cutting the candied cherry in two and place one half at each end. Instead of cherries, you can use orange peel or chopped pistachios. Top it with a generous sprinkling of powdered sugar and serve

THE STORY

Behind My Recipe

The celebration of Carnevale is the Italian version of Mardi Gras in New Orleans with oranges instead of beads. Many of the biggest celebrations are on Martedi Grasso or Fat Tuesday. Celebrations are held all over Italy from Venice and Milan down to the villages and towns of Sicily. During the celebrations, which can last from a day to a month, revelers are free to eat, drink, and dance without reproof.

Of course, Carnevale would not be complete without food. The word carnevale derives from the Latin "carne vale" or farewell to meat. As Ash Wednesday approached, people were obliged to fast. In the south of Italy and especially around Naples, the end of Carnival on Fat Tuesday, is celebrated by eating Lasagne di Carnevale or Lasagne alla Napoletana.

"Chiacchiere" is a typical sweet of the Italian Carnival. The origins of this dessert date back to the ancient Romans, who used to prepare fried sweets (named "frictilia") during the Saturnalia celebrations (a festivity which is comparable to today's Carnival). Chiacchiere are made throughout Italy, but their name varies from region to region: for example, they are called crostoli in Trentino, sfrappole in Bologna, cenci in Tuscany, and bugie in Liguria.

CHIACCHIERE

SERVES 4

INGREDIENTS

- 3 cups + 2 tbsp white flour
- 4 eggs
- 1/2 tablespoon of sugar
- 1 pinch of salt
- ¼ cup butter
- 1 shot glass of Spirit
- peanut oil for frying
- Icing sugar

INSTRUCTIONS

- Knead the flour together with four eggs and a half tablespoon of sugar. Add the softened butter, a pinch of salt and a shot glass of spirit, and knead by hand until the dough is smooth and not too hard. Cover it with a kitchen towel and let it rest for about an hour. Meanwhile, heat the peanut oil in a pan with high sides and sprinkle a little bit of flour on the work surface and the rolling pin.

- After the rest, roll the dough out with the rolling pin until it is very thin. Now, using an indented wheel, cut the strips 10-12cm long and 1cm wide and twist them into different shapes. As soon as the oil is sizzling, dip the strips and turn them until they are golden-brown on both sides. At this point, remove them from the oil and leave them to drain on a sheet of kitchen roll. Finally, sprinkle the chiacchiere with abundant icing sugar.

PIGNOLATA

Pignolata is a dessert only made in the southern part of Italy, made for Christmas. We coat them with an orange blossom honey and cinnamon

INGREDIENTS

Sicilian Style For the Dough
- 3 ½ cups flour
- 1 teaspoon baking powder
- 1 tablespoons sugar
- 4 tablespoons salted butter (½ stick) soft at room temperature
- 2 large eggs
- ¼ cup of Marsala or 2 tablespoons of liquor (cognac, vodka, etc.)
- Flour for dusting

INSTRUCTIONS

- Mound flour on a flat surface and form a well or use a bowl. Mix into the well the butter and the sugar, then break the eggs, beat with a fork and add the Marsala. Start to blend the flour from the inside of the well and keep incorporating the flour; add a few drops of water, if needed, to moisten the flour. Using your hands, bring all the flour together to form a ball with the dough. Fold and press with the palm of your hands; if the dough is sticky, add some more flour. When the dough forms a single mass, set aside. Clean your hand and working surface and discard scraps.

- Dust the working surface with flour and knead the dough by pushing it down firmly to the center; turn the dough 90 degrees and press down again: keep kneading until the dough is elastic and has a silky consistency. Knead for 4-5 minutes. Cover and rest dough for 20/30 minutes. Divide dough into 3 pieces and roll out each piece of dough with a rolling pin ½ inch thick. Cut into strips about ½ inch. Roll and stretch each strip in the form of a breadstick about ¼ inch thick and cut into ¼ inch, to form small balls.

COOKING INSTRUCTIONS
PIGNOLATA

- **For Frying**

Canola or corn oil for frying. Heat a heavy duty pan with the oil at least 1 inch deep. When oil reaches about 375 degrees, start to fry the balls. When the pignolata is golden (not brown) on all sides, transfer the little pastries to drain into a dish covered with paper towels.

- **The Finishing**

In a small saucepan combine the sugar, zest of orange and 1 cup of water. Bring to a boil and simmer for 3 minutes. In a large saucepan warm up the honey and add the sugar syrup. Mix it well. Add the strufoli and using a wooden spoon turn until they are well coated with the honey and syrup mixture. Place the little balls in a serving dish piling up in the shape of a pine cone and dust it with grounded cinnamon. The pine cone in Sicilian is called pignu hence the name pignulata.

FOR THE ICING

- ½ lb orange blossom honey
- Zest of 1 orange
- 2 tablespoons of sugar
- Grounded cinnamon

FOR THE CHOCOLATE ICING

- 2 cups granulated sugar
- 12 oz. baking bitter cocoa
- 1 cup of water
- 3 drops of vanilla
- ½ teaspoon powdered cinnamon for dusting

FOR THE LEMON ICING

- 1 lb. confectioners sugar
- Juice of 5 lemons
- Zest of 5 lemons
- 1 tablespoon granulated sugar for dusting.

TORTA CAPRESE

Torta Caprese is a dark chocolate cake made without any flour. This specialty of the Italian island of Capri consists of dark chocolate, eggs, sugar, almonds, and butter. It is characterized by its dense chocolate texture and a layer of powdered sugar on top.

TORTA CAPRESE

SERVES 8

INGREDIENTS

- 1 ⅓ cups almond flour (or meal)
- 4 ½ ounces chocolate, chopped (bittersweet or semi-sweet)
- ½ cup each: salted butter and granulated sugar
- 3 large eggs, room temperature (and separated)
- 2 teaspoons vanilla extract
- powdered sugar, for dusting

INSTRUCTIONS

- Line an 8-inch round cake pan with parchment paper, set aside. Position a rack in the center of the oven and preheat the oven to 325ºF. Place the chopped chocolate in a glass bowl, along with the butter and heat in the microwave in 30-second increments until the butter melts. Make sure to stir in between.

- You'll want to stop before the chocolate melts completely. Let sit for a few seconds then start stirring, the hot butter helps melt the chocolate without additional microwave zaps! When the chocolate melts, add the sugar and the almond meal and stir. Allow the mixture to cool to the touch. Then add the egg yolks and the vanilla extract; stir to combine.

- In the bowl of an electric mixer fitted with a whisk attachment, beat the egg whites until soft peaks form. Fold the whites into the chocolate mixture, gently so you don't knock all the air out.

- Pour the batter into the prepared cake pan. Smooth out the top and bake for roughly 36-39 minutes or until the top sets and a skewer inserted in the center comes out mostly clean (crumbs are fine, you don't want wet batter though.) Allow the cake to cool completely in the cake pan (set over a wire rack.) Dust the cake with powdered sugar before serving with whipped cream or fresh fruit!

RICOTTA CHEESECAKE WITH PINEAPPLE

PINEAPPLE RICOTTA FILLING
- 3 large eggs
- 1 cup sugar
- 1 cup heavy cream
- 1 tbsp vanilla extract
- 1 tbsp cornstarch
- 1 pound ricotta cheese drained well, using fine mesh strainer
- 16 ounces crushed pineapple drained well, using fine mesh strainer

PIE CRUST
- 1 ¼ cup all purpose flour
- ¼ cup sugar
- ½ teaspoon salt
- 5 tbsp unsalted butter cut into cubes
- 1 large egg
- 1 tbsp grated lemon from one small lemon
- ½ teaspoon (½ teaspoon) baking powder

INSTRUCTIONS

DECORATING THE PIE
1 tbsp cinnamon powder

MAKE THE PIE CRUST
- Add sugar, flour, salt, baking powder, and cubed butter in a large bowl. Using your hands, incorporate the butter into the dry ingredients until the mixture looks like coarse sand.
- In another bowl, lightly whisk the eggs and then pour into the dry sand-like mixture and stir until all of the egg has been incorporated.
- Press down, form a dough, and knead a few times until no dry bits remain. Form a flat disk shape, wrap in plastic wrap, or place into an airtight plastic bag and refrigerate for at least 1 hour.

MAKE THE PIE FILLING
- Beat the eggs, sugar, and cream until blended.
- Add vanilla and cornstarch and mix until combined.
- Add ricotta and mix slowly.
- Fold in the pineapple and slowly mix until incorporated.
- If you're not ready to bake, place the filling in the refrigerator. Cover with plastic wrap to prevent skin from forming.

INSTRUCTIONS
SERVES 12

BUILD THE PIE
- Grease a 8 or 9 inch baking pan with cooking spray or butter.
- Remove the pie crust from the refrigerator and roll out into a circle that is about 12 inches in width, using plenty of flour to coat the countertop and top of the pie crust. Add more flour and flip the crust at least one or twice as you are rolling it out. I find a bench knife or scraper helps me to lift the crust when I want to flip it. See link in notes section for more tips. You may want to trim the outer edges to make a neat circle using a pizza cutter or knife. It may help to drape the pie crust over the rolling pin when you are transferring it to your baking pan. Line the baking pan with a pie crust and form a decorative edge. Place crust into the refrigerator while you warm up the oven.

BAKE THE PIE
- Preheat the oven to 425 degrees (you will later reduce the temperature to finalize baking). Place one rack on the second to lowest position and another in the middle of the oven.
- Remove pie crust from refrigerator and pour in the prepared filling.
- Filling should be at least ¼ inch or so below the top of the pie crust.
- I used tin foil to protect the edges of the pie from burning. See blog post for a photo of what this looks like.
- Bake the pie at 425 degrees for 15 minutes. After 15 minutes, reduce oven temperature to 325 degrees and bake for an additional 50 to 60 minutes. For the first 30 minutes of baking, bake on the lower rack and then move to the middle rack for remaining back time. The pie will puff up a bit but still be a little jiggly but not overly so. After the pie has slightly cooled, sprinkle it with cinnamon powder if desired. Store pie in the refrigerator until ready to serve.

TETÙ AKA MEATBALLCOOKIES

The weeks before Christmas Day our family baked cookies, fruitcakes, and prepped a lot of food. There were two cookies, Tetù and Lemon Ricotta Cookies that I adored as a child and continue to make during the holidays as an adult.

We called this cookie "meatballs." They are round and dark brown, like a meatball. Tetù or Sicilian Chocolate Spice Cookies are rich, dense chocolate cookies flavored with allspice, nutmeg, warm spices and orange zest. Tetù are traditionally prepared on All Saint's Day (November 1st) in Sicily or during the Christmas holidays in North America.

TETÙ AKA MEATBALL COOKIES

SERVES: 6 - 8

Storage: Store at room temperature in an airtight container with non-stick or wax paper between the layers for 5 days. Freeze in an airtight container for up to one month. When thawing, don't remove instead thaw cookies completely in the container.

INGREDIENTS

- 2⅓ cups all (plain) purpose flour
- ⅓ cup unsweetened cocoa powder
- 2 ½ teaspoons baking powder
- ¼ teaspoon salt
- ½ teaspoon cinnamon
- ¼ teaspoon freshly ground nutmeg
- ¼ teaspoon allspice
- 2 large eggs
- ½ cup sugar
- ½ cup extra-virgin olive oil
- ½ cup milk
- 2 teaspoon vanilla extract
- ¾ cup walnuts chopped medium fine
- 1 cup mini choc chips

ICING

- 1 ½ cups powdered sugar
- 1 tablespoon milk or more if necessary
- Sprinkles for decorating
- Mix the powdered (icing) sugar and milk together to form a thick but spreadable icing. Add more milk if needed.

INSTRUCTIONS

- Preheat the oven to 350ºF/160ºC and line two large baking trays with non-stick baking paper.

- Whisk (or sieve) together flour, cocoa, baking powder, spices and salt. With a whisk attachment on an electric mixer, beat together eggs until frothy then slowly add sugar. Beat until pale and thick. Slowly drizzle in the olive oil followed by milk and vanilla.

- Using a wooden spoon, add the flour mixture in two lots, stirring until smooth. Stir through the walnuts and mini choc chips. The dough will be soft and sticky. Cover the bowl with plastic wrap and allow the dough to rest for 20 to 30 minutes.

- Take rounded teaspoonfuls of the dough and roll between your palms into a ball. Place the balls on the prepared trays allowing room for spreading and rising.

- Bake for 10-12 minutes. Don't over bake - these are meant to be soft and moist. The cookies will rise and form a few cracks. Cool on the trays for a few minutes before transferring to wire racks to cool.

- Spread a small amount of icing on each cookie and decorate with coloured sprinkles. Allow icing to set before serving or storing.

ITALIAN RICOTTA COOKIES

MAKES 30 COOKIES

Storage: Store at room temperature in an airtight container with non-stick or wax paper between the layers for 5 days. Freeze in an airtight container for up to one month. When thawing, don't remove instead thaw cookies completely in the container.

INGREDIENTS

- 2 c. all-purpose flour
- 1 1/2 tsp. baking powder
- 1/2 tsp. kosher salt
- 1/4 c. (1/2 stick) butter, softened
- 1 c. granulated sugar
- 8 oz. ricotta
- 1 tsp. pure vanilla extract
- 1/2 tsp. almond extract (optional)
- 1 egg

ICING

- 1 c. powdered sugar
- 2 tbsp. whole milk
- 1/4 tsp. almond extract (optional)
- Sprinkles
- Whisk together the powdered sugar and milk until smooth. Whisk in the almond extract, if using. Spoon the icing over the cookies, and top with sprinkles while the icing is still wet.

INSTRUCTIONS

- Make the cookies: Adjust an oven rack to center position and preheat the oven to 350°. Line 2 baking sheets with parchment paper. In a medium bowl, whisk together the flour, baking powder, and salt. Set aside.

- In the bowl of a stand mixer fitted with the paddle attachment or in a large bowl with a hand mixer, cream together on medium speed the butter and sugar until light and fluffy. Add in the ricotta, vanilla, almond extract, if using, and egg and continue to mix until smooth. (The batter will be quite wet.)

- Add the dry ingredients and mix just to combine. Portion the dough into approximately 1½ tablespoon portions (or use a medium cookie scoop) onto the parchment spaced 2" apart. Bake for 15 minutes. (The tops will remain pale while the bottoms turn golden brown.) Cool the cookies on a wire rack with parchment paper underneath.

PASTIERA NAPOLETANA

(Traditional Neapolitan Cake)

No Neapolitan Easter meal would be complete without pastiera on the table. It is made with whole wheat berries, cooked in milk until creamy, and mixed with ricotta, sugar, eggs, candied citrus, and orange blossom essence for the filling. Families all over Naples begin making this on Thursday or at least the Friday before Easter – soaking the grains in water and then boiled in milk until tender. It is worth all the time and work.

INGREDIENTS

- 4 cups of all-purpose flour
- 11 oz. of lard
- 1 2/3 cups of sugar
- 8 of large eggs
- 2 cups of milk
- 21 oz. of sheep's milk ricotta cheese
- 9 oz. of uncooked wheat berries
- 1 stick of unsalted butter, plus extra
- 4 oz. of candied citron and orange, diced
- 1/2 packet of vanillin
- 1/2 vanilla pod
- orange blossom extract
- zest of 1 lemon
- 1 tsp. of ground cinnamon
- salt
- zest of 1 orange

INSTRUCTIONS

- Cook wheat berries in boiling water for 2 hours. Drain and cook with milk and 1 tsp. cinnamon, a little orange zest and 1/2 vanilla pod until the milk is absorbed (around 15 minutes); alternatively you can use 1 lb. pre-cooked wheat berries (grano cotto); heat in 1 cup milk along with the other ingredients for 10-15 minutes. Let cool.

- In a large bowl mix flour, lard, 2/3 cup sugar and a pinch of salt until it resembles breadcrumbs. Add 2 eggs and mix with your hands until combined. Use your hands to shape the dough into a ball. Place in the refrigerator in a bowl sealed with plastic wrap for at least 30 minutes. Preheat the oven to 340 °F.

- Mix the ricotta with the rest of the sugar, adding it a little at a time. Separate 2 eggs and set the egg whites aside. Beat yolks with the ricotta mixture. Add 4 whole eggs, one at a time, and whisk until incorporated. Add a little lemon and orange zest, candied fruit and 2 Tbsp. orange blossom water. Remove the vanilla pod from the cooked wheat. Beat the egg whites until stiff and fold into the ricotta mixture along with the cooked wheat. For a creamier filling purée some of the cooked wheat berries.

RECIPE

- Grease and flour a 10" cake pan, preferably a springform pan. Roll out about 2/3 of the dough on a floured surface until it is about 1/4" thick. Place in the springform pan. Cut off any overhang to add to the remaining dough. Roll out remaining dough and cut into 10 strips around 1" wide.

Fill the dough with the ricotta mixture. Lay the pastry dough strips across the top in a criss-cross diamond pattern. Press the strips gently to adhere on the edge of the pastry. Bake for 1 hour and 30 minutes until golden. Remove from the oven and let cool for at least 8 hours in a dry place.

Meet The Chef

Chef Margie Raimondo's roots in her culinary career were planted at a young age. Both parents' families immigrated from Italy to an urban community in south Los Angeles, where most of the sources of their food were the rabbits and chickens they raised and the vegetables they grew in the yard of their urban house. As an adult, she always planted a seasonal garden with herbs and vegetables for her kitchen. In 2014 after a 20-year marketing career in Silicon Valley, she moved to Italy to broaden her culinary skills by living on farms and learning more about farming, food preservation and production.

When she returned home to Little Rock, she planted her first seeds at Urbana Farmstead, a one-acre urban farm that grows seasonal vegetables, fruits, and herbs to sell in her market and to make fresh, prepared meals and preserves. Her menu is inspired by the ever-changing seasons which gives her healthy and nutrient-dense whole food to transform into delicious food. Urbana Farmstead Market is more than a market for farm produce. It offers specialty foods from Italy and other artisan producers, extra virgin olive oils, and freshly baked bread. Visiting Urbana Farmstead is reminiscent of Chef Margie's childhood days, filled with artisanal ingredients, seasonal farmer's market produce and authentic Italian hospitality. When she is not in the kitchen or the garden, she writes about the intersection of food, agriculture and farming. Her genre is heritage food and farm storytelling through film and cookbooks.

This book is dedicated to all the family and friends who shared their favorite recipes and cooking tips with me.

Special thanks

To my loving partner, Chris Beaver,
for taking this journey of life with me.

My two children, Jennifer and Amy
four grandchildren, Aidan, Logan, Blake, and Brooklyn
along with my two fur babies, PJ and Nola.

MANGIAMO

MEDITERRANEAN FAMILY RECIPES

GET IN TOUCH

www.urbanafarmstead.net
www.raimondostudio.com

 URBANFARMSTEAD

 MARGIE RAIMONDO

www.ingramcontent.com/pod-product-compliance
Lightning Source LLC
Chambersburg PA
CBHW060535010526
44119CB00005B/162